THE WORD FOR THE WORLD

The Word for the World

**Growing as a Christian
with John's Gospel**

Volume 1: John chapters 1 – 6

*Stephen Gaukroger
with Simon Fox*

Crossway Books
Leicester

ISBN 1–85684–122–7

Scripture used in this work, set in italic type, is taken from
the New International Version of the Bible, Copyright ©
1973, 1978, 1984 by the International Bible Society.
Published in Great Britain by Hodder & Stoughton Ltd.
The author's own paraphrases and amplifications of biblical
passages have been set in roman type within quotation
marks.

Typeset by Avocet Type, Brill, Aylesbury, Bucks.

Printed in Great Britain for Crossway Books,
38 De Montfort Street, Leicester LE1 7GP,
by Cox & Wyman Ltd, Reading, Berkshire.

CONTENTS

Introduction   1
1. Jesus, the Word of God   5
2. Two baptisms   15
3. Meeting Jesus   23
4. Gullible or cynical?   29
5. A miracle at a wedding   37
6. Cleansing the temple   49
7. The new birth   55
8. Marks of maturity   69
9. Breaking down barriers   75
10. Jesus' method of evangelism   81
11. Three lessons to learn   91
12. Do what the Father does   101
13. Divine resources   109

INTRODUCTION

John was one of the twelve disciples chosen by Jesus. So what we have in the Gospel of John is not an account written by some idle spectator who was not really involved in the events described. This gospel was not written by someone who turned up on the scene, rather like a journalist, asking people what happened and then reporting second-hand facts. John was actually there, seeing everything at first hand.

These days many people receive the teletext services on their televisions. It's remarkable how quickly the news stories are included on the news pages of Ceefax and Oracle. They enable you to keep right up to date with the news, twenty-four hours a day. But there is a small time-lag between the event happening and the report of it getting on to the teletext pages.

However, there is no time lag at all in John's Gospel. It wasn't that someone told someone who told someone who told someone who told John. He was actually there! He was called by Jesus to be one of the original proclaimers of the gospel. This is an eye-witness account from someone who walked with Jesus, talked with him, sat down to evening meals with him and chatted over the events of the day with him. John would have said to Jesus, 'What were you doing with that blind man this morning?' And Jesus would have answered, 'Well, I healed him, and I did it like this … And when I've gone and the Holy Spirit comes you will be able to do the same thing, and it will happen like this ... and like this ...'

We all know that Jesus had twelve disciples. But John was not just one of the Twelve: he was one of the Three. The Three were Peter, James and John, the closest friends of Jesus. He had realized that he couldn't share himself fully with as many as twelve, so he chose three men out of the twelve to be his intimate confidants. In effect he was saying to them, 'I am going to share my life with you even more deeply, intimately and fully than with those other nine. I am going to share with you my principles of living, my principles of power.'

Chapter 9 of Mark's Gospel tells the story of the Transfiguration, in which Jesus takes these three men up a mountain, where they have an amazing experience: the glory of God descends upon Jesus, his clothes become dazzling white, and they see him somehow talking with Elijah and Moses, two of the Old Testament prophets. Only these three disciples had the privilege of seeing that great event, and John was one of them.

And not only was John one of the Three, but he was also the disciple who was closest to Jesus. In John 13:23 we read that at the Last Supper John, *the disciple whom Jesus loved, was reclining next to him.* In the ancient world people didn't eat at a table, sitting on chairs. Instead they ate lying down in a circle, leaning on one elbow. So John would have been lying next to Jesus, and they would have been able to talk about things quietly and intimately while they were eating together. Jesus shared some very important truths with John, his close friend, and John wrote them down for us so that we too can know Jesus personally.

Mark's Gospel was the first of the four gospels to be written. It is short, pithy and to the point; it has no long explanations. It is full of action and life. Then Matthew's Gospel was written especially for the Jews who needed a lot of explanations about Jesus. They knew all about Yahweh, the great God of the Old Testament, but who was this Jesus person? Then there was Luke's Gospel, which was written for the Gentiles, who had never heard of either Yahweh or Jesus and who needed a factual account of Jesus' life. That's why the story of his birth is fuller in Luke than in any other gospel. Luke was explaining to the Gentiles who Jesus was and where he came from. John's Gospel was the last to be written (perhaps at around AD 80), and it was an attempt to say to the world, 'This is what Jesus means.' It is a gospel of explanation, a gospel of purpose. There are only eight miracles recorded in John, while there are dozens in the other gospels. John isolates each miracle and makes a point out of it and says, 'This is who Jesus is, this is why he came into the world.'

If you are not yet a Christian or have only recently become one, there is no better place to begin learning about Jesus than in John's Gospel. Even if you have been a Christian for decades, there are truths in this gospel which will amaze you.

Chapter 1

JESUS, THE WORD OF GOD

*In the beginning was the Word, and the Word was
with God, and the Word was God. He was with
God in the beginning.*

  *Through him all things were made; without him
nothing was made that has been made. In him was
life, and that life was the light of men. The light
shines in the darkness, but the darkness has not
understood it.*

(John 1:1–5)

John's Gospel opens with the words, *In the beginning was
the Word* ... Who is this Word? Verse 14 of the same
chapter tells us that

*The Word became flesh and made his dwelling among us. We
have seen his glory, the glory of the One and Only, who came
from the Father, full of grace and truth.*

So this tells us that the 'Word' which verse 1 refers to is
Jesus.

Now why does John use the term 'Word' here? Why
doesn't he just say, 'In the beginning was Jesus ...'?
John's Gospel was originally written in Greek, and the
term which is translated into English as 'Word' is the
Greek word *logos*. To the ancient Greek philosophers
the *logos* was the ground of all being. To them it
symbolized thought, ideas, and all that was best in
everything. John took the idea of the *logos* and gave it a

whole new meaning. In effect he was saying, 'You may think that the Word is a great idea, but I'm telling you that God's greatest idea, God's greatest thought and plan was Jesus. Jesus Christ is the *logos.*'

Moreover, by referring to the Word John is not only speaking to the Greeks, but is also speaking to the Jews. How did God create the world? Genesis chapter 1 tells us that he did it by speaking.

God said, 'Let there be light,' and there was light … And God said, 'Let there be an expanse between the waters to separate water from water'… And God said … 'Let dry ground appear' … Then God said, 'Let the land produce vegetation …'

and so on. God made things happen with a *word.* God spoke the universe into being. If he had remained silent nothing would have happened. So the Word is evident back in Genesis 1. John is saying that the Word, God's self-expression, is not only to be seen in the creation of the universe: the greatest expression of God is Jesus Christ.

The eternal Jesus

In the beginning was the Word … and the Word was God.

(John 1:1)

The term 'beginning' here translates the Greek word *archē*, which means 'the originator, the original, the very beginning', and it picks up on an idea from the Old Testament Hebrew word *bara*, which means 'created out of nothing'. God has given us the gift of creativity: we may be artists or writers or musicians or carpenters or sculptors or engineers: using various kinds of raw materials, we can design and create things. But when we create, we do it out of *something.* We have to have a raw material to start with: we cannot create out of *nothing.* Only God can do that. He not only 'designed' and 'sculpted' the universe, but he also created the raw matter from which he made everything.

So before there was anything at all, God existed. John tells us that *In the beginning was the Word, and the Word was with God.* In other words, Jesus was with God before time itself began. Jesus is eternal, and there was nothing before him. In the book of Revelation he says,

I am the Alpha and the Omega … who is, and who was, and who is to come, the Almighty … I am the First and the Last.
(Revelation 1:8, 17)

'Alpha' is the first letter in the Greek alphabet and 'Omega' is the last: Jesus is the very beginning and the very end.

Sometimes there is a tendency for Christians to be somewhat blasé and casual about the God they worship. We don't worship a tin-pot little god who has existed for a long time, we worship a God who has *always* existed. There was nothing before Jesus – nothing at all: no earth, no moon, no sun, no planets, no stars, no galaxies. This is a crucial truth to get hold of: we need to know and believe that the Jesus whom we love and serve is God the Son in eternal relationship with God the Father.

John 1:3 tells us that through Jesus *all things were made; without him nothing was made that has been made.* It's thrilling to think that all the wonderful world we see around us was made through Jesus. He was the agent of creation. I have travelled by air quite a lot, and it's amazing to travel at 30,000 feet and see the world spread out below you. Sometimes you can see entire cities, or mountain ranges or forests or mighty rivers. There is amazing variety and beauty in the world, and yet it isn't all a fluke or accident; it didn't happen by chance. It was designed and made by the Father, in co-operation with Jesus.

In [Jesus] was life, and that life was the light of men. The

light shines in the darkness, but the darkness has not understood it.

(John 1:4–5)

As the years go by different names for children become fashionable and others go out of fashion. In the past five years or so names like Zac, Tristan and Kylie have become popular. Another fashionable name at present is Zoe. In fact this name is the Greek word for 'life', and it is the word used here in John's Gospel: in Jesus *was* zoe, *and that* zoe *was the light of men.* In John 10:10 Jesus says, *I have come that they may have* zoe, *and have it to the full.* What he means by this lovely statement is that in him and in him alone there is real life, true life, eternal life, life in a new dimension – Life with a capital L.

But apart from Jesus there is no real life at all. Jesus is *the light* which *shines in the darkness.* When you bring a candle into a dark room or switch on a lightbulb, the light instantly banishes the darkness. In the battle between light and dark, the light always wins; it is irresistible. Jesus said,

I am the light of the world. Whoever follows me will never walk in darkness, but will have the light of life.

(John 8:12)

He is saying to us, 'I have come into this world, which was dark with sin and evil, but as soon as I stepped into the world I dispelled all the darkness with my light, and the darkness cannot extinguish it. Nothing can blow my candle out. It's not possible. Take it or leave it, like it or lump it, my light is going to shine, for I am the Light of the World.'

What this means is that until we become Christians, until we receive Jesus into our lives, we have no real life in us. All we have is physical life: we are the biological result of a sperm and an ovum coming together, producing a human being. Now, I don't wish to seem arrogant or proud in saying this, as if Christians are better than non-Christians, but the Bible tells us very clearly that in Jesus there is life and light, but apart from Jesus there is only death and darkness. If you have not yet become a Christian, you are still in death and darkness. Every human being needs to find Jesus, to discover his life and light; only then will you find out who he really is, and only then will life become something real and worthwhile to you. And those of us who are already Christians need to be reminded that beyond Jesus there is no real life or light; true fulfilment and joy can come only from him. He longs to bless us and change us, to make us truly new people in him.

The Word became flesh

The Word became flesh and made his dwelling among us. We have seen his glory, the glory of the One and Only, who came from the Father, full of grace and truth.

(John 1:14)

This verse can be misleading for some people, since the word *flesh* suggests the literal flesh upon our bones. However, that isn't what John's Gospel is talking about here. By the phrase *The Word became flesh* John is saying that Jesus, the Son of God, took on human form: he became a human being with a human body. He did this in order to reveal himself to us, identifying with us, so that his death could bring about our salvation.

John describes Jesus as *The One and Only* Son of God. He is the unique one, the singled-out one, the one without whom there is no life or light. Why is there no light or life without him? Because he is the only Son of God: there is no other son of God to whom we can turn for light and life.

The amazing thing is that this unique Son of God *became human,* and because of that he understands everything about us. Those of us who have been

Christians for quite a while may know this in our heads, but it may not have registered in our hearts. Jesus lived as a human being almost two thousand years ago, and because he lived that human life he knows at first hand, from the inside, as it were, what it is like to be human. Many people suffer terrible stress and anxiety about their work or their home life; but in some amazing way, because Jesus was human, he understands that suffering. Some women have to endure discomfort in their monthly cycle, and for some this is an intensely unpleasant experience: in addition to the physical pain, there can be powerful emotional disturbance. But somehow Jesus understands all that; he knows all about our suffering and our mood-swings. If we are Christians, we are never alone: Jesus always understands what we are going through and is always there to comfort us.

Not only does Jesus *understand* our problems, but he also has the *power* to do something about them. He wants us to tap into his power; he wants to revolutionize our lives, flooding them with his light and life.

Jesus is the unique Son of God. There is no-one else like him; he is indispensable. However, the same cannot be said about us. We need to remember that none of us are indispensable. There is absolutely no reason for us to be proud or arrogant. There is no room in the Christian life for a conceited self-assurance about what we say and do. Jesus is great and wonderful, the eternal Creator God, the author of life and light; compared with him, we are nothing. John the Baptist said about Jesus,

He *is the one ... the thongs of whose sandals I am not worthy to untie.*

(John 1:27)

We need to have John the Baptist's attitude. We need to understand clearly that God is the Sovereign Lord; we should not think that we are more important than we really are. Whatever work we are doing for God, he could probably achieve results just as good, or even better, through someone else. Jesus is the only one who cannot be replaced. We are simply his servants, and we are only of use to him if we are humble before him.

Recognizing Jesus

[Jesus] *was in the world, and though the world was made through him, the world did not recognise him. He came to that which was his own, but his own did not receive him.*

(John 1:10–11)

I find that a very sad statement. Jesus had made the world, and yet when he came into the world as a human being, the world (that is, people) did not know who he was. He went about doing miracles, healing sick people, raising the dead to life, restoring sight to blind people, making deaf folk hear again, curing people of leprosy, speaking his wonderful good news … and yet, most people couldn't or wouldn't see that he was the Son of God.

Nothing has changed. Now, at the end of the twentieth century, preachers stand up in pulpits Sunday after Sunday, talking about this marvellous Jesus who is alive today, and still people don't recognize him. There is a veil over their eyes. They can't see who Jesus really is: their Saviour and their Lord. The world of the first century wasn't ready for Jesus, and the world today is no different.

So first of all we need to *recognize* Jesus for who he is.

Receiving Jesus

However, there is another side to the story: there have always been some people who have accepted Jesus,

Yet to all who received him, to those who believed in his name, he gave the right to become children of God.

(John 1:12)

11

So, having recognized Jesus, we need to *receive* him into our lives.

Jesus is the Son of God, so when we receive him we too become children of God, with Jesus as our great Elder Brother, with his life flowing into us, changing us, developing us, blessing us.

When I'm in America I love to watch the TV programmes there, especially the commercials, which I find very amusing (even the ones which aren't meant to be funny!). 'How would you like to earn a million dollars a year?' was the beginning of one of the adverts. And then it explained how this could come about, if only I would send So-and-So Inc. twenty dollars without delay! Most of us have dreamed sometimes about being rich. We might fantasize that we are the son or daughter of a multi-millionaire, able to travel to all sorts of exotic places, to have all the things we want and to do all the things we really want to do. But the truth is that as Christians we *really are* the sons and daughters of the best, richest, most famous, most powerful person who has ever lived! We *are the children of God*.

He has built mansions of glory for us – not just in heaven, but here on earth too! He wants us to explore and enjoy them, but sadly, many of us never enter the mansion but instead live in the dog-kennel outside. God is saying to us, 'I have made you my sons and daughters with a marvellous inheritance. I have given you a wonderful birthright. Why are you still living in that dog-kennel? Dog-kennels are for dogs. Children belong in a proper home. Please will you leave the kennel and enter your mansion?' God wants to open up for us the great horizons of divine sonship and daughterhood so that we will experience all the glory that he has prepared for us. I am increasingly aware that there is so much of God that I have not yet experienced, and I am desperate to know more of what it is to be a son of the great King, to be filled with his power, and to have my birthright as a child of God.

Reflecting Jesus

There came a man who was sent from God; his name was John. He came as a witness to testify concerning that light [i.e. Jesus], so that through him all men might believe. He himself was not the light; he came only as a witness to the light. The true light that gives light to every man was coming into the world.

(John 1:6–9)

The Greek word translated *witness* here can also mean 'martyr'. To be a martyr – to die for your faith – is the ultimate form of witnessing, and in the end John the Baptist did indeed become a martyr. John was not himself the light; he was merely the mirror which reflected the light. People came to him and asked if he was the Christ, or Elijah, or the Prophet (*i.e.* Moses), but he denied being any of them. All he had to say about himself was,

I am the voice of one calling in the desert, 'Make straight the way for the Lord'.

(John 1:19–28)

He was saying, 'I am the one who shouts about the light, I am the mirror who reflects the light.' He reflected glory and status away from himself and directed everyone's attention towards Jesus.

We are called to do the same as John the Baptist did. Having recognized and received Jesus, we must *reflect* him: by the way we live we should say to the world around us, 'Come and experience the light and life which is available for you in Jesus! When you do, you will become a son or daughter of God, the heavenly King!'

Chapter 2

TWO BAPTISMS

The next day John saw Jesus coming towards him and said, 'Look, the Lamb of God, who takes away the sin of the world! This is the one I meant when I said, "A man who comes after me has surpassed me because he was before me." I myself did not know him but the reason I came baptising with water was that he might be revealed to Israel.'

Then John gave this testimony: 'I saw the Spirit come down from heaven as a dove and remain on him. I would not have known him, except that the one who sent me to baptise with water told me, "The man on whom you see the Spirit come down and remain is he who will baptise with the Holy Spirit." I have seen and I testify that this is the Son of God.'

(John 1:29–34)

The Lamb of God

This is a very exciting passage. It tells us a little more about who Jesus is and a lot more about what Jesus wants to do in all our lives, whether we have just been converted or we have been Christians for a long time.

In verse 29 of our passage John the Baptist calls Jesus *the Lamb of God* and he refers to him by the same title in verse 36. In the New Testament Jesus is given a variety of different titles, such as Saviour, Lord, Christ, Messiah, King, Son of God and Son of Man. Lamb of God is one of those titles, and behind it is a rich

15

background which the Jews to whom John the Baptist was speaking would have understood instantly.

There are certain things in our modern television culture which ring instant bells with us. If I were preaching a sermon and I said it was designed to refresh the parts that other sermons cannot reach, my listeners would (I hope) chuckle, and they would instantly think of the commercials for a certain well-known brand of Dutch lager. Of course, if the sermon had been taped and I used a time-machine to send the tape back thirty years to 1964, the people hearing it would merely think I was a bit strange! And if I were to send the tape forward to 2024, the people then would probably not have the faintest idea what I was talking about. Similarly, the title *Lamb of God* does not have the impact on us today which it would have had on John the Baptist's audience. 'Yes,' we may say to ourselves, '"Lamb of God" is a nice title for Jesus, but what does it actually mean?'

At the mention of the Lamb of God, the minds of John's hearers would have been instantly drawn back to the book of Exodus, to that momentous event in their national history known as the Passover (Exodus chapters 11–12). God had already inflicted nine plagues upon Egypt, but still Pharaoh would not let the Israelites leave his kingdom. Consequently God had to send a tenth plague, the plague on the firstborn: every firstborn son among the Egyptians was going to die. He had warned the Israelites about this and had told them to sacrifice lambs and to paint the blood of the lambs on the lintels of their doors. If they did this, the angel of death would pass over their houses and none of them would die. So the tenth plague came: the Egyptians were decimated but the Israelites were unharmed, since they were protected by the blood of the sacrificial lambs.

So in calling Jesus the Lamb of God John the Baptist

is saying that Jesus is the sacrificial Lamb whom God has provided to protect his people from death. But the Lamb of God is infinitely greater than the lambs of the Passover: Jesus will save God's people not merely from physical death but from *eternal death* and will bring them to *eternal life* : by his blood he will wash away their sins and make them righteous before God. They will still have to die physically, but they will be saved by the Lamb from spiritual death.

In Old Testament times people had to offer animals as sacrifices to God in order to say sorry for their sins. But Jesus, the Lamb of God, was the ultimate sacrifice: after he had been sacrificed on the cross for our sins, there was no longer any need for animals to be sacrificed. Jesus put an end to the old system of sacrifices: we only need to look to him as our sacrifice so that we can have forgiveness of sins and eternal life.

Jesus was the Lamb of God back in the first century, and he is still the Lamb of God today. His sacrifice of himself on the cross is as effective for us as it was for the people of his own day. All we need to do is accept the sacrifice he has made: we have to be truly sorry for our sins, and Jesus' sacrifice will cover our wrongdoings and wash them away. Whatever sins we have committed this week or today – for example, bad temper, gossiping or greed – Jesus is the sacrifice whose blood can cleanse us from them all. We don't need to go out to the local park and sacrifice some animals – Jesus is all the sacrifice we need. This is a thrilling truth, once we clearly see it and get hold of it.

Water-baptism and Spirit-baptism

John the Baptist said,

The one who sent me to baptise with water told me, 'The man on whom you see the Spirit come down and remain is he who will baptise with the Holy Spirit'.

(John 1:33)

So John baptized with water, but Jesus was going to baptize people with the Holy Spirit. John's baptism symbolized repentance:

And so John came, baptising in the desert region and preaching a baptism of repentance for the forgiveness of sins.
(Mark 1:4)

But the baptism in which Jesus baptizes people is a baptism in *power*, in reality – a baptism in the Holy Spirit. In other words, it is not merely a symbolic action with water; on the contrary, it brings about a dramatic change in someone's life. Of course, it is not the water itself which is powerful, or even the act of being sprinkled with it or submerged in it! The power comes from God as a result of our obedience and willingness to receive.

It is sadly the case that for many years the baptism in the Holy Spirit was something which was utterly untaught in most churches. As a result many Christians experienced only a John-the-Baptist kind of baptism, a baptism of repentance. No-one had ever mentioned the power of the Holy Spirit to them. No-one had ever told them that they could be filled with the Spirit's power, that they could receive and exercise his gifts. They were told, 'Well, when you become a Christian you make a commitment to Jesus, and you get baptized, and that's that.' But that isn't what the New Testament teaches us about baptism; it shows us that baptism should be at one and the same time symbolic of repentance (*i.e.* baptism in water) *and* powerful (*i.e.* baptism in the Holy Spirit).

People often get worked up about the timing and terminology of baptism in the Spirit. Do we get baptized in the Spirit before water-baptism, or during it, or afterwards? Does baptism in the Spirit happen six months after water-baptism, or ten years after? The Bible is gloriously imprecise about all this!

For example, in the book of Acts there is the account of Peter's preaching to a large gathering of people in the house of Cornelius:

While Peter was still speaking these words, the Holy Spirit came on all who heard the message.

(Acts 10:44)

Peter and his Jewish friends who had come with him were amazed at what had happened, since the people who had been baptized in the Spirit were Gentiles and had not even been baptized in water. Peter said,

Can anyone keep these people from being baptised with water? They have received the Holy Spirit just as we have.

(verse 47)

To take another example, there is the incident in Acts 19:1–7 where Paul, arriving in Ephesus, met some believers and asked them,

'Did you receive the Holy Spirit when you believed?' They answered, 'No, we have not even heard that there is a Holy Spirit.'

Paul then asked them what baptism they had received, and they replied that they had had John's baptism. Paul explained to them that John's baptism was merely a baptism of repentance, and so Paul then baptized them into the name of the Lord Jesus.

When Paul placed his hands on them, the Holy Spirit came on them, and they spoke in tongues and prophesied.

So in our first example the people received baptism in the Spirit before baptism in water, and in the second example the men had water-baptism before Spirit-baptism. Is the Bible wrong here? Did Luke, in writing down these accounts, get the order of events mixed up in one of them? No, not at all. What this apparent confusion tells us is that the order in which these

19

things happen is not of crucial importance. God doesn't work in a rigid, legalistic pattern: first A must happen, then B, then C, then D ... What really is important is that the *symbol* which is water-baptism must be accompanied at some stage by the *reality* which is Spirit-baptism. In other words, a baptism in water tends not to have a significant effect on an individual's life unless Jesus is also present in his power, baptizing the person in the Holy Spirit. If that real spiritual power is lacking, a water-baptism is merely a matter of taking a bath in public! Baptism needs that inner dynamic of the Holy Spirit if it is to be what God intended it to be: a life-changing event.

So there is no point in arguing about whether some experience we had yesterday or a week ago or six years ago was baptism in the Spirit or the fullness of the Spirit or being filled with the Spirit or whatever we want to call it. The timing isn't very important and neither is the terminology. But what is important is that we should be *filled with Christ*, no matter when or how. We need to experience the spiritual reality of which water-baptism is a sign.

In America a number of years ago some Christians formed a group called the Full Gospel Businessmen's Fellowship. They used the phrase 'Full Gospel' because they felt that so much of the mainstream church was preaching and living only part of the gospel: that is, the outward, symbolic, intellectual, churchgoing part of the Christian life. The churches lacked the power of the Holy Spirit. The charismatic movement has very rightly reminded us all that Christianity is not just about head-knowledge, but also about spiritual reality. Many Christians need desperately to be more aware that their *experience* of Jesus Christ should correspond to their *knowledge* about him. Too many of us are just going through the motions of what it means to be a Christian. Duty is a valid part of the Christian life, but there is more to being a Christian than duty. We need to obey God's commandments, but there is more to Christianity than that. We need to study the Bible and apply it to our lives, but there is more to Christianity than that. Some church traditions are good and important, but there is more to Christianity than tradition. We need to have a personal relationship with God, who longs to baptize us in his Holy Spirit.

The Greek word *baptizo* originally meant completely immersing a piece of cloth in a dye, so that when you take the cloth out it is a totally different colour. Being baptized in the Spirit should have that sort of effect on us: we should have a new colour altogether! We need to move on from going through the motions of Christianity to spiritual reality. We need not just the symbolic baptism but also the baptism in the power of the Spirit. And only Jesus can give us that baptism, as God told John the Baptist:

The man on whom you see the Spirit come down and remain is he who will baptise with the Holy Spirit.

(John 1:33)

Chapter 3

MEETING JESUS

The next day John was there again with two of his disciples. When he saw Jesus passing by, he said, 'Look, the Lamb of God!'

When the two disciples heard him say this, they followed Jesus. Turning round, Jesus saw them following and asked, 'What do you want?'

They said, 'Rabbi' (which means Teacher), 'where are you staying?'

'Come,' he replied, 'and you will see.'

So they went and saw where he was staying, and spent that day with him. It was about the tenth hour.

Andrew, Simon Peter's brother, was one of the two who heard what John had said and who had followed Jesus. The first thing Andrew did was to find his brother Simon and tell him, 'We have found the Messiah' (that is, the Christ).

And he brought him to Jesus. Jesus looked at him and said, 'You are Simon son of John. You will be called Cephas' (which, when translated, is Peter).

(John 1:35–42)

Salvation in Jesus

Here we see Jesus at the beginning of his ministry, bringing salvation to John, Andrew and Peter. First of all John and Andrew followed Jesus and spent that day with him (we are not actually told that John was one of the two disciples mentioned in verses 35–39, but it is hard to see how it could be anyone else). Then Andrew went off and told his brother Simon that he and John had found the Messiah. 'Messiah' is the Hebrew equivalent of the Greek word 'Christ', and they both mean 'the Anointed One', the one sent from God, the one who has come to accomplish something for God, to be the Saviour of God's people.

In this passage there is a lovely phrase which makes it obvious that this is a personal, eye-witness account: verse 39 says, *It was about the tenth hour* when John and Andrew first met Jesus. The Bible commentaries tend to disagree over what *the tenth hour* means. If it was the tenth hour in Roman time, it would have been ten o'clock in the morning; if it was Jewish time, it would have been four o'clock in the afternoon. No-one really knows for sure which is correct, but that doesn't matter. What does matter is that the writer of the gospel was remembering this event, which was the crucial turning-point in his life. At the tenth hour on that particular day he met Jesus for the first time and saw who he really was.

Similarly, many Christians today can say precisely when they first met Jesus – when for the first time they understood who he really is and gave themselves to him and received him as their Saviour. It may have been at a Billy Graham crusade, or at a church service, or at a youth meeting, or in their own home, or in their car, or out in the country while going for a walk. Some people are able to say things like, 'I became a Christian while I was mending my car at 3.30 p.m. on Wednesday the 12th of October, 1985.' However, many other Christians, like myself, are not able to specify a precise time or place. They became a Christian over a certain period of time: it may have been days, weeks, months or even years. They can't say on what day it happened, but they can say that at the start of that period they did not know who Jesus was and they did not understand the gospel, but at the end of the period they knew that Jesus was their Lord and Saviour.

A 'gradual conversion' is just as real and valid as a 'quick conversion'. What matters is not when or how it happened, but *has it happened?* The issue is not when you began walking with Jesus, *but are you walking with Jesus now?* Many times I have met elderly Christian folk who tell me that they were converted at an evangelistic crusade sixty or seventy years ago, and you can see that their lives are still radiant with Jesus: they have loved him and walked with him ever since their conversion. But I also meet people who were converted in 1920 or whenever, and after talking with them for a while it becomes clear that since that initial commitment they have not really walked with God: through all those years they have made little spiritual progress.

John, the writer of the gospel, was one of those who could name the precise time of his conversion: it was the tenth hour on such-and-such a day, and after that experience he followed Jesus faithfully.

Witnessing about Jesus

So we have thought about what it means to have salvation in Jesus the Messiah. The next thing which this passage in John's Gospel shows us is the importance of witnessing to other people about Jesus:

The first thing Andrew did was to find his brother Simon and tell him, 'We have found the Messiah.' ... And he brought him to Jesus ...

(John 1:41)

Jesus' method of evangelism was *Come, and you will see* (verse 39), or 'Come and see, and you will find out.' So Andrew came and saw, and he found out that Jesus was the Messiah. He then went and fetched Simon, and Simon too came and saw and found out, and in due course Simon himself would bring many people to come and see Jesus. This is the basic message of evangelism: 'Come and see! Come and meet Jesus, come and share the salvation which I have found in him.'

I am absolutely convinced that the Christian gospel is completely reasonable and rational; biblical Christianity is intellectually and academically defensible. So we should not be afraid of getting into arguments and debates about our faith: Christianity can be rationally defended against any other worldview. I am quite happy to sit down with anyone who sincerely wants to discuss Christianity from an intellectual point of view. However, my basic evangelistic technique is not to subject people to a five-hour-long lecture on the reasonableness of Christian belief. Generally speaking, people do not come to faith in Christ by that approach; intellectual argument and debate, although vitally important as a step on the way, rarely gets people into God's kingdom. Most people come to faith in Jesus Christ because someone has said to them, 'I have found something and I want you to find it too.' Jesus has become real to them, so they want to share him with other people, and so others come to know Jesus in a wonderful domino effect. What we need to do is to witness about Jesus, to share him with other people – we cannot argue them into the kingdom. Now, of course, once people have committed themselves to Jesus, they will often need to think things through and they will have some questions which they want answered, so that is the time for making their faith intellectually understandable. However, a meeting with Jesus must come first.

Commissioned by Jesus

We have thought about salvation in Jesus and witnessing about Jesus. The third thing which this passage shows us is the commissioning which Jesus gives us.

Jesus gave a commission to Simon Peter. Andrew

brought [Simon] to Jesus. Jesus looked at him and said, 'You are Simon son of John. You will be called Cephas'.

(John 1:42)

All the names in this passage have some kind of significance. Rabbi means 'teacher'; Jesus means 'saviour'; John means 'beloved' or 'prince'; Andrew means 'manly' and Peter means 'rock'. Jesus was saying to Peter, 'I want to commission you: I am sending you out in my name, and you will no longer be Simon but the Rock.' Elsewhere Jesus says to him,

I tell you that you are Peter, and on this rock I will build my church.

(Matthew 16:18)

Jesus called Peter the Rock because he knew that this man would be the firm, solid foundation which the church would need.

Jesus wants to commission all of us, and part of that commissioning is being given a new name. When we are born physically as babies, our parents give us a name. Similarly, when we become Christians, this is such a big change in our lives that it is like being born again. God has re-created us and given us his spiritual gifts and authority, and spiritually we receive a new name, a new identity. Scripture shows that in Jesus we have many new names. God says to us, 'I have made you a new person; I have given you a new identity. I have given you the name Christian: live up to that name. I have named you Follower of Christ, Child of God, Beloved of the Father: live up to those names. I have named you Joint Heir with Christ, which means that you can have everything I gave to Jesus: live up to that name. I love you. All this blessing is for you. I want you to have it and take it. I want you to live in the fullness of the inheritance I have given you.'

Chapter 4

GULLIBLE OR CYNICAL?

The next day Jesus decided to leave for Galilee. Finding Philip, he said to him, 'Follow me.'

Philip, like Andrew and Peter, was from the town of Bethsaida. Philip found Nathanael and told him, 'We have found the one Moses wrote about in the Law, and about whom the prophets also wrote — Jesus of Nazareth the son of Joseph.'

'Nazareth! Can anything good come from there?' Nathanael asked.

'Come and see,' said Philip.

When Jesus saw Nathanael approaching, he said of him, 'Here is a true Israelite, in whom there is nothing false.'

'How do you know me?' Nathanael asked.

Jesus answered, 'I saw you while you were still under the fig-tree before Philip called you.'

Then Nathanael declared, 'Rabbi, you are the Son of God; you are the King of Israel.'

Jesus said, 'You believe because I told you I saw you under the fig-tree. You shall see greater things than that.' He then added, 'I tell you the truth, you shall see heaven open, and the angels of God ascending and descending on the Son of Man.'

(John 1:43–51)

Nathanael asked, *Nazareth! Can anything good come from there?* Nazareth was a kind of by-word in Judea at that time. It was regarded as an inferior place, the sort of town you would not visit unless you really had to. In most cities today there will be one or more districts which have a bad name. If you are moving in to the city, people will tell you, 'If I were you I wouldn't think of buying a house there,' referring to the local suburb which everyone loves to hate. 'It's got a terrible crime rate and the people are very rough.' When I was a teenager living in Preston in Lancashire the local no-go area was a particular district of Merseyside. It had a dreadful reputation. I'm sure it must have been an exaggeration; I expect this area wasn't really any worse than most other suburbs of big cities. Nazareth was the no-go town of Judea! It seemed incredible to Nathanael that the Messiah could come from such a place. Shouldn't the Messiah come from somewhere impressive, like Jerusalem? But Nathanael did not understand that this was part and parcel of Jesus' divine humility. He had voluntarily humbled himself by becoming a human being, by being born in a mere stable, by growing up in the much-despised town of Nazareth.

Stop pretending!

When Jesus saw Nathanael approaching he said of him, 'Here is a true Israelite, in whom there is nothing false.'

(John 1:47)

In other words, Jesus was able to sum up Nathanael immediately. Nathanael didn't need to say or do anything to show what kind of a man he was: Jesus could see his true character straight away.

One of the things which comes across very clearly in John's Gospel is that there was no fooling Jesus. He effortlessly saw through every pretence, façade and barrier which people erected. There is still no fooling him today. He sees right through us and knows what you and I are really like. All of us act in life: we try to fool God, other people and even ourselves by trying to pretend that we are something that we're not. We may pretend to be more spiritual than we really are, because we want to impress people in our church. Or we may try to pretend that we are less spiritual than we really are so that our non-Christian friends won't think we're boring and stuffy. We get involved in all sorts of little acting games.

But Jesus is the one person we can never fool, because he sees right through us. I don't say that as a threat, to make the people reading this book feel exposed and guilty and foolish. In the past I have heard preachers threaten their congregations with the thought that God knows everything about them, and so don't they feel terribly guilty and sinful? One could see the people squirming and sweating with anxiety! I'm saying this not as a threat but as a comfort. Jesus knows everything about us, so let's just stop pretending that we are something we aren't and let's just relax in his love for us. We don't need to play our silly little games with him; he only wants us to be ourselves. Sometimes when we pray by ourselves Jesus will say to us, 'Now wait a minute; stop pretending. Be honest with me and with yourself. Be real with me so that I can minister to you.'

When I was a youth leader in my church in Preston a fifteen-year-old lad joined our group. He had just become a Christian and came from a completely pagan background, so he didn't know anything about prayer. Unfortunately he had received some very unhelpful teaching about prayer, and so his first attempt to pray at one of our meetings was very embarrassing for him and for the rest of us! He simply read out a prayer which someone had written down for him, and it seemed to be worded in seventeenth-century English! It began with the words, 'We thank thee, O Lord, that our sojourn here is not long ...' This poor lad had been told by some rather traditionally-minded Christian that this was the correct way to pray! I'm sure God must have been shouting in heaven, 'Forget all that stuff! My son, just talk to me – be real, be yourself. I will understand what you're trying to say!'

Once we take the step of being honest with God and ourselves, the fact that we can't fool him is wonderfully liberating. There is no need for pretence with God. All Christians are free to be themselves. There is no need to copy anyone else. There's no need to dress up or dress down when you go to church on a Sunday; just wear what you feel comfortable in. We don't need to pretend that we are something we are not, and we don't have to try to fit into a standard Christian mould. God loves us and wants us to be ourselves, in love with him.

Having said that, yes, it is true that God makes certain demands of us. When our lives get out of line morally he will tell us to get back on track. And he wants us to be continually changing so that we increasingly resemble him. But he wants us *really* to become better Christians, not to pretend that we are better than we are.

Gullible Christians

Nathanael was convinced that Jesus was the Messiah when Jesus told him that he had seen him while he was still under the fig-tree before Philip called him (John 1:48). Only God's Anointed One could have such amazing supernatural knowledge. So Nathanael is prepared to trust Jesus when faced with incontrovertible proof that he is the Messiah. He has a trusting attitude, but he is not gullible. We know that from his remark in verse 46, doubting that anything good could come from Nazareth. He was not prepared to believe that Jesus was the Messiah just because Andrew had told him that he was. Nathanael wanted more proof than that. There is a big difference between faith and trust on the one hand and gullibility on the other hand.

Unfortunately it must be said that there are quite a lot of gullible Christians around these days. I have frequently been staggered to see otherwise sensible Christians accepting something at face value simply because they have read it in a Christian book. The fact that someone has written something and it has been published does not necessarily mean that it is true or right. The Bible tells us that in the last days certain 'prophets' will arise who will preach all sorts of lies which will mislead even some of God's people: gullible Christians will believe what they say and wander away from the truth without stopping to ask themselves whether the message they have heard is based on God's Word. We need to have a sound knowledge of Scripture so that we can check against it whatever we read or hear. If something we read in a Christian book clearly contradicts God's Word, we should reject what we have read in that book. If it doesn't actually contradict Scripture but still seems a bit odd, it is wise to discuss the matter with a mature Christian.

Many of the Christian books which give people's personal testimonies are excellent and well worth reading, but others, while not actually telling untruths, only tell part of the truth. Sometimes they leave out the unpleasant side of the story: they tell you only about the glory and not about the pain which had to be gone through in order to reach it.

Cynical Christians

So gullibility is one of the undesirable extremes which Nathanael avoids. The other extreme he avoids is that of cynicism, which today is, if anything, an even greater problem than gullibility among Christians. Faced with indisputable evidence that Jesus is the Messiah,

Nathanael doesn't beat about the bush; he puts his trust in Jesus. Sadly, there are many Christians today who lack his willingness to believe. With respect to the miraculous or something new and dynamic in church life their attitude is, 'That will never happen. It's never happened in all the years I've been a Christian. Surely you can't really believe that! Yes, I know the Bible promises it, but I've never seen it happen, and it's probably never going to happen. Yes, I know Jesus promised it, and yes, I know we had a miracle in the church last week, but it won't happen again. You can't count on these things; it won't amount to anything in the end. Things will just carry on pretty much as normal, you'll see!'

This sort of attitude has become a deeply ingrained part of Christian thinking in this country. The worldview of our modern age, which tends to reject anything supernatural and miraculous, has crept into the church and established itself very securely. The result is that vast numbers of Christians are paralysed by cynicism and unbelief. It is no wonder that many churches today are dead and powerless!

The pervasive cynicism of the British church becomes acutely apparent to me when I return to this country after spending some time in the USA. Some of the American Christians have an outlook which is completely free of cynicism. In Britain we usually say, 'Why should we do it?' but in the States they say, 'Why shouldn't we do it?' We say, 'We've never done that before – so we can't do it now'; they say, 'We've never done that before – so let's get on and do it now!'

Dubious theology has eaten the heart out of British Christianity. People no longer believe the Word of God. People say, 'We can't believe Genesis, because it's too simplistic; we can't believe Revelation, it's just nonsense; half of the Old Testament is unbelievable; the miracles in the gospels didn't actually happen; the book of Acts is surely one big exaggeration; Romans is too complicated; Corinthians is too easy ...' and so on. The end result? We are left with a Bible which is only three pages long! Let's commit ourselves to rejecting the spiritual cancer which this doubtful theology has produced.

How do Christians become cynical? Often it's through being hurt. In the past they have been somewhat gullible, usually with the best of motives; they have trusted someone or some sort of ministry that was not trustworthy, and as a result they were disappointed, disillusioned and hurt. So in order to protect themselves from being hurt that way again they become cynical: they become reluctant to trust anyone or any teaching wholeheartedly. They cover their emotions over with a cynical veneer. God longs to release people from that kind of bondage and to bring them into a faith which is alive and fresh and vibrant.

Let us reject the spiritual sickness which is cynicism. Let us also be aware of the need to grow out of gullibility and to become spiritually mature. Let's embrace the Nathanael kind of faith: a faith which is wise and mature and yet trusting and genuine.

Chapter 5

A MIRACLE AT A WEDDING

On the third day a wedding took place at Cana in Galilee. Jesus' mother was there, and Jesus and his disciples had also been invited to the wedding. When the wine was gone, Jesus' mother said to him, 'They have no more wine.'

'Dear woman, why do you involve me?' Jesus replied, 'My time has not yet come.'

His mother said to the servants, 'Do whatever he tells you.'

Nearby stood six stone water jars, the kind used by the Jews for ceremonial washing, each holding from twenty to thirty gallons.

Jesus said to the servants, 'Fill the jars with water'; so they filled them to the brim.

Then he told them, 'Now draw some out and take it to the master of the banquet.'

They did so, and the master of the banquet tasted the water that had been turned into wine. He did not realise where it had come from, though the servants who had drawn the water knew. Then he called the bridegroom aside and said, 'Everyone brings out the choice wine first and then the cheaper wine after the guests have had too much to drink; but you have saved the best till now.'

This, the first of his miraculous signs, Jesus performed at Cana in Galilee. He thus revealed his glory, and his disciples put their faith in him.

(John 2:1–11)

Miraculous signs

We actually know very little about this wedding which took place at Cana in Galilee. We don't know who the bride and groom were, we don't know who the parents were, and we don't know who the guests were, apart from Mary, Jesus and his disciples. Since Jesus and his mother were invited, the bride or the groom may have been a relative. The writer, John, would have been there and so he would have known all the facts, but he chose to exclude them from the account. I believe he did this because he wanted to make sure that the true significance of this incident was not obscured by unnecessary details. What matters is what Jesus did, not what colour the bride's dress was!

And what Jesus did was this: a *miraculous sign* (verse 11) in a very ordinary situation. Obviously, it was a very special day for the bride and groom, but it was just a simple country wedding, of a kind that would have been happening all the time all over Judea. The embarrassed host of this wedding encountered a very human, ordinary problem: the wine had run out! It was a catering disaster, nothing more. And yet Jesus intervened and by his divine power turned the water in the jars into superb wine. Suddenly this ordinary little wedding was turned into something very special and wonderful. It became a life-changing event for the people there: they had never seen anything like this before! It was a turning-point for Jesus' disciples:

He thus revealed his glory, and his disciples put their faith in him.

(verse 11)

Miraculous sign is the New International Version's translation of the original Greek word *semeio*, which literally means 'sign'. There are eight such signs in John's Gospel. A sign is a thing which points towards something else. When we're driving down a motorway and we see a sign saying 'London 35', we don't get out of the car and go and look at the sign thinking, 'So that's London, is it?' No, the sign tells us which way to go and how far to go, and we keep on driving until we get there. Likewise, the miracles in John's Gospel are signs. They are not very important in themselves: they point to something else.

In the next chapter Nicodemus says to Jesus,

no-one could perform the miraculous signs you are doing if God were not with him.

(verse 2)

So the miraculous signs show us that God is with Jesus: they show us that he really is the Son of God. In other words, in the New Testament signs and wonders are an integral part of evangelism. In the gospels and in Acts we see them being used to point people to Jesus Christ: they saw the divine power being exercised by Jesus or by his disciples, and so they were convinced that he was the Messiah and believed in him.

I believe that one of the reasons why the church of Jesus Christ in the UK is so ineffective in its evangelism is that it lacks the miraculous dimension. The church today needs to work towards demonstrations of God's power and authority: then people will be pointed towards Jesus, as they were in the first century. God's principles of operation never change. Much of our evangelism is skilfully worded; we are clever at explaining the gospel to people. But then, having heard our words, the people we are evangelizing look at our personal lives, they look at our churches, they look at our way of doing evangelism, and they compare all this with the Bible, and they notice a huge difference. The church was filled with God's power in New Testament times, but where is the power in the church today?

I believe that Christians today should pray that God

will move in their lives and in their churches in power, so that the world may see that God is real and alive and means business today. The heart of the Christian message is that the Jesus of the gospels who went around healing sick people, raising the dead, casting out demons and giving salvation and hope and joy to people is alive today and is still doing the same things. That is what we need to be saying to a world which is totally lost and misguided without Jesus, which seems unaware of who he is, which seems unable to see him at all. It is good to talk about Jesus, but that is not enough: unless the church today demonstrates Jesus' authority as it did in New Testament times, we will face a very uphill struggle in our evangelism. Christians need to be excited about the potential for Jesus' miraculous power to be released into people's lives today. We should expect to see God's supernatural power being expressed in our church services, in our home groups, in our prayer meetings, in our Sunday schools, in our youth groups.

We should expect demonstrations of the miraculous – *not demonstrations of emotionalism*. These are two totally different things. There are far too many 'revival' meetings which try to get everyone worked up emotionally, as if emotion alone will make miracles happen. In the gospels, things happened the other way round. First, Jesus worked a miracle, and *then* the people got excited about it. What we want is real miracles, not emotionalism: we want to see *God* work, not just human psychology and biochemistry. So we need to pray that God will work in our churches in supernatural power, and when he answers that prayer, *then* we can get excited about it!

We need to make sure that our basic attitude about the miraculous is right. We should want miracles so that through them people will be convinced that Jesus is the Son of God, and so that people will be healed

40

and blessed. We should be careful that we are not desperate for the miraculous simply because we enjoy being excited. God performs miraculous signs for his own glory; he does not do miraculous tricks for our entertainment. If we want miracles merely so that we can be thrilled and we can brag about it to our friends in other churches, we are making the miracle more important than Jesus, the one who is doing the miracle, and such an attitude is idolatry. Our motives for wanting miracles must be pure: we must want miracles so that Jesus is uplifted and honoured and glorified; we must want miracles which will point to Jesus in all his splendour.

Water into wine

Jesus did something wonderful at the wedding at Cana: he turned mere water into delicious wine. This is a powerful picture of what he wants to do for every single person on the face of this planet. He wants to transform the dull water of our lives into the sparkling new wine of his presence. This wine imagery occurs many times in Scripture. In Acts chapter 2, the disciples are all gathered in the upper room and suddenly the Holy Spirit comes on them with a mighty, rushing wind and tongues of fire, and they all speak in strange new languages. They must have made a lot of noise, because people out in the street overheard all this, and some of them made fun of the disciples, saying, *They have had too much wine.* But Peter told them,

These men are not drunk, as you suppose. It's only nine in the morning!

(Acts 2:15)

And he went on to explain to them that he and the other disciples had been filled with the Holy Spirit. So the effect of being filled with the Spirit seemed to the onlookers to be like drunkenness – the disciples were

41

enjoying the wine of the Spirit. This is what God wants for Christians: he wants us to be filled with the bubbling new wine of his power.

Sadly, many Christians seem not to have tasted the new wine and have merely sampled sour grapes. It is true to say that if a non-Christian lived with some of us for any length of time they would get the strong impression that being a Christian is all about being miserable. This is tragic, because that is not what God intended. Christianity is meant to release within us Jesus' new wine – a life of divine joy and energy.

It's important to remember that the Jews and the other people of the ancient world did not drink wine in quite the way we drink it. Wine was not an expensive drink for special occasions but was a regular part of a family's diet and lifestyle. One of the reasons for this was that water supplies were often contaminated, and so water by itself would not have been safe to drink. So wine was mixed in with the water to sterilize it. So the wine they would have drunk at the wedding party at Cana would probably have been diluted with water. The people were drinking wine because it was a pleasant thing to do to celebrate a happy family occasion – they didn't drink in order to get drunk. This was not a wild, Bacchanalian party but an enjoyable family gathering in which the wine was a sort of social lubricant. So that is the picture of the Christian life which the image of new wine suggests to us: something wholesome, joyful, healthy and happy.

If you have committed your life to Jesus, I urge you not to settle for dull, stale water but to long for the wine of Jesus' presence – this is the bubbling, sparkling experience which God wants you to have. Don't accept water when you can have his wonderful wine; don't make do with the ordinary and mediocre when Jesus can transform the ordinary as he did at Cana and turn it into something amazing. Far too many Christians have settled for mediocrity in their lives and are drifting along from one dull experience to another, when all the time God wants them to be filled with the new wine of his presence and power.

Do whatever he tells you

Mary, Jesus' mother, said to the servants at the wedding,

Do whatever he tells you.

(verse 5)

That little sentence is the key to this miracle. If the servants had ignored what Jesus had told them to do there would have been no miracle. If they had not filled the jars with water, it would not have been turned into wine. But, amazingly, they did as they were told. As they gave a sample of the wine to the master of the banquet they may well have been quaking in their boots, expecting to lose their jobs for giving him plain water, and yet they still obeyed. The result was a wonderful miracle.

Mary knew that in order for something marvellous to happen, Jesus had to be obeyed, and so she told the servants to follow his orders. The same is still true today: if we obey Jesus, miracles will start to happen, simply because we are getting into line with what he wants to do.

Some Christians like to have Scripture verses prominently displayed in their homes as reminders of important truths about God and the Christian life. One of the favourite verses is 'Do whatever he tells you.' Unfortunately, in some homes wives have placed a picture of their husband near this verse, so that visitors get the mistaken impression that the verse refers to the wife's obedience to her husband! But, of course, the 'he' who is being referred to is Jesus. Obeying Jesus is crucial to our spiritual growth.

There are some things which the Bible clearly tells us are wrong: for example, murder, adultery and theft. However, there are many other things in life which the Bible doesn't tell us about specifically. So these things may be right for some people in some circumstances, but they may be wrong for other people in other conditions. So Jesus may want Joe Bloggs to be a missionary, but that does not mean that his friend Dave Smith should do the same: God may want Dave to carry on working as a postman so that he can be a Christian witness in his workplace. God has different plans for each of us about the details of life. We should all be faithful to our marriage partners, but we don't all get called to the mission field. All of us need to listen carefully to God and do *whatever he tells us to do.*

If we obey him, the result will always be the best thing for us: the best thing for our marriages, for our families, for our careers, for our businesses, for our work for God. If we don't obey him, we will always be choosing the second best. This may not always be obvious in the short term, but in the long term it is clear that God's way is always the best way for us. One of the reasons why there is friction in Christian homes, churches, organizations and businesses is often that the people involved have never actually asked Jesus what he wants. A decision has to be made, and the people consider it and weigh up the alternatives and finally go for one of them, without taking the trouble to ask God what he wants them to do. They may well end up making a decision which is out of line with his will, and the result is that things don't go well, and so problems and friction are created.

Often we make decisions on the basis of what our neighbours or our in-laws or our friends at school or work or church will think. There are many forces influencing us as we try to make decisions: there are many people who think that we should listen to their opinions, who think that we should try to fit in with their wishes and expectations. But ultimately the only thing that matters is that we should do what Jesus wants us to do: really his voice is the only one we need to listen to. If Jesus is telling us one thing and people are telling us something else, then we must obey Jesus and disappoint the people, rather than vice versa. Now, of course, that does not mean that we should refuse to listen to others. Often Jesus will show us his will partly through the advice of mature Christians (and also through wise non-Christians whom we respect). But we should be listening to what *Jesus* has to say *through* them.

This is one of the wonderful privileges of being a Christian. Christian living isn't just going through life with our heads stuffed full of biblical principles and commandments: being a Christian is to have a personal relationship with Jesus. Because he is the Son of God he knows everything about us – indeed, he knows us far better than we know ourselves – and he knows everything about the world in which we have to make our way. Not only that, but he loves us and wants what is best for us. So if we give the control of our lives over to him, we will be far better off than if we are trying to control things ourselves, because Jesus is infinitely wiser and infinitely more powerful than we are.

At the end of John chapter 2 we read these words:

Now while he was in Jerusalem at the Passover Feast, many people saw the miraculous signs he was doing and believed in his name. But Jesus would not entrust himself to them, for he knew all men. He did not need man's testimony about man, for he knew what was in a man.

(verses 23–25)

Jesus had absolutely no illusions about how sinful and unreliable fallen human nature is. Jesus was not willing to entrust himself to the people, because he knew he could not depend on them. He knew that the very same people who were now saying, 'Jesus is wonderful! Look at the amazing miracles he is doing!' would one day turn against him. As he made his triumphal entry into Jerusalem he must have known that the very same people who were then greeting him enthusiastically and saying, *Blessed is the King of Israel!* (John 12:13) would later say, *Crucify! Crucify!* (John 19:6). The same people who were now applauding his miracles would later want him dead. Jesus knew all about the fickleness of the human heart. He keenly appreciated the difference between the people who saw a miracle and responded emotionally, and the people who saw it and responded with commitment to him, wanting to stick with him through the bad times as well as the good times. There were many people in Judea who would have eagerly accepted the chance to become Jesus' disciples. But Jesus chose very carefully indeed: he called only twelve men, and even they were a pretty mixed bunch! Indeed, one of them, Judas Iscariot, eventually betrayed him to the religious leadership. There were only three men in his 'core team' – Peter, James and John – and even Peter denied Jesus after he was arrested.

God calls us to a faith which is based not on superficial, temporary emotions but on a commitment to Jesus which will go through any kind of trial and emerge from it triumphant. God is calling us away from easy believism – the sort of attitude which says, 'Yes, I'll be a Christian as long as everything goes well, but when the going gets tough I'll drop my Christian commitment.' This is fair-weather Christianity: 'Yes, Lord, we'll do your will, but we'll do it only when we feel like it, only when it doesn't conflict with all the other things we want to do. Yes, Lord, we'll make doing your will a priority – priority number ten, that is. You see, there are these nine other things we want to do first. Once we've done them, we'll do your will. Yes, Lord, we'll follow you anywhere you want us to go – unless, of course, you ask us to go there ... or there ... or there. You can't expect us to go to places we don't like!'

Do whatever he tells you (John 2:5) should be our motto, but it isn't easy to have that sort of attitude. It is no small thing to be really willing to do whatever God wants us to do. That sort of obedience is not something we can arrive at in an instant. We will need to work at it for a long time. When I was twenty-one and was about to go to Spurgeon's College as a single man, I had to do some serious thinking and praying about my future life. By opting to go into the ministry I was effectively excluding a lot of other possibilities in my life, and I was struggling in prayer to commit all of this to God. One of the things I was committing to God during this period was the question of marriage or singleness. When I was fourteen I had gone to a Christian conference at which the speaker had said that we teenagers should start praying right then about whom we should marry. So I had prayed about it ever since then, but that had been seven years ago, and in the intervening time I hadn't met any young lady who seemed to me like the future Mrs Gaukroger! Eventually I got to the point where I knelt beside my bed and prayed, 'Lord, if you want me to be single for the rest of my life, then I will be.' I stood up again, but two seconds later I was back on my knees praying, 'Lord, I don't mean that!' In my heart of hearts I was not willing to remain single, so I realized that it wasn't right to tell God that I was willing. I had to be honest with him. I was unable to say, 'Lord, whatever you want is fine by me,' because I did not feel able to go without a wife for ever. For most of us it takes years of openness with God to get to that point.

I get worried when people make public professions

to the effect that they are willing to do anything God wants them to do and are willing to go anywhere he wants them to go. Often they don't realize the magnitude of the commitment they are making; are they really willing to do something that does not appeal to them? Are they really willing to go somewhere they don't like the sound of? Praying that sort of blanket prayer of obedience to God can be a dangerous thing to do. We should only pray it if we really mean it. God does not want a superficial commitment based on a passing emotional high; he wants commitment which is honest, realistic and aware of the possible consequences of obedience. He wants us to be real with him.

Chapter 6

CLEANSING THE TEMPLE

After this he went down to Capernaum with his mother and brothers and his disciples. There they stayed for a few days.

When it was almost time for the Jewish Passover, Jesus went up to Jerusalem. In the temple courts he found men selling cattle, sheep and doves, and others sitting at tables exchanging money. So he made a whip out of cords, and drove all from the temple area, both sheep and cattle; he scattered the coins of the money-changers and overturned their tables. To those who sold doves he said, 'Get these out of here! How dare you turn my Father's house into a market!'

(John 2:12–16)

The traditional, cosy image of 'gentle Jesus, meek and mild' is not a true reflection of his character, as this story vividly illustrates. Jesus was not a quiet, unassuming soul who was afraid to risk offending anyone. He was not a sort of first-century equivalent of our modern politicians at election time, going around kissing babies and trying to make everyone like him. On the contrary, he was a strong, vigorous, courageous man who had the guts to stand up to hypocrisy and injustice and sin when he encountered it.

Crooked trading

It's important to understand the background to this

incident. All devout Jews had to pay a temple tax, and that tax could only be paid in shekels, the Jewish currency. So the people came to the temple wanting to pay their tax, but since shekels were only one of the currencies in use in Judea – there would have been Roman coins, Greek coins, you name it – they would often not have enough shekels. That was the purpose of the money-changing tables. The people would hand over their foreign coins in return for Jewish shekels, at whatever the current rate of exchange happened to be. Originally this practice had been perfectly legitimate. In return for their services the money-changers had charged a small commission, which was fair enough, since they had to make a living. But over the years the system had become corrupted, until by Jesus' time the commission charged was greater than the money exchanged. For example, to change one shekel you may have had to pay a commission of two shekels. This was absolutely outrageous, especially since the poor could not afford it. This was why Jesus was angry with the money-changers. He was saying to them, 'You have twisted something legitimate and useful and made it into something which robs the poor! You have betrayed the trust given to you!'

The selling of sacrificial doves had also been corrupted. The doves sold in the temple were much more expensive than those sold elsewhere, and the people were obliged to buy the temple doves because only they were ever passed by the temple inspectors as being good enough to offer as sacrifices. Whenever anyone offered a dove which had not been bought at the temple, it was invariably declared unfit for sacrifice, even though there was absolutely nothing wrong with it.

So the money-changers and dove sellers were ripping people off left, right and centre. Jesus was so angry about this that he made a whip and drove out all the sheep and cattle and turned over the money-changers' tables. Money would have rolled about all over the place. Jesus turned the temple upside down! That is hardly the behaviour of a 'gentle Jesus, meek and mild'! By his action Jesus was saying, 'I will not have God's temple used to exploit the poor! The temple stands for holiness, decency and integrity, and yet you have turned it into a place of dishonest exchange!'

Jesus was not saying that the temple was holy ground as such: he was saying that it was a place reserved for holy worship of God. It was not the place itself which mattered, so much as the activity which went on inside it, and clearly crooked trading was totally beyond the pale. The same is true of our churches today. The buildings themselves are not the focus of holiness, because holiness is something which is related to people and not to material things. A building is made sacred and holy by the Christians who worship God in it. What Jesus will not tolerate is dishonesty and hypocrisy taking the place of true worship. He wants lies and hypocrisy to be rooted out of our fellowships and out of our individual lives. The Bible says,

Do you not know that your body is a temple of the Holy Spirit?
(1 Corinthians 6:19)

Each Christian is a temple of God, and God does not want there to be things in the temple which should not be there – the spiritual equivalents of crooked money-changers and dove salesmen. Jesus wants all of the sinful rubbish cleared out of our lives so that we are pure and wholesome temples of God in which Jesus alone reigns supreme.

Double standards

It is easy for us to fall into the trap of double standards. Many Christians live a pagan kind of life from Monday to Saturday and suddenly become wonderful

Christians on Sunday. They may have been working with the same people for years, and yet their workmates have never found out that they are Christians because they lead a double life. That sounds a very hard thing to say, but I am afraid it is true for more Christians than we would like to admit. How many Christian husbands say things at work which they would never say in the hearing of their wives? How many parents put on special behaviour when their children are around but behave differently when the kids are at school or in bed? So many of us put on acts and pretend all sorts of things. Jesus is calling us to throw all the rubbish out of the temple and to lead lives of integrity and wholesomeness.

Everyone knows what I am referring to when I talk about the Real Thing. A few years ago there were almost riots on the streets of America when the Coca Cola Company tried to introduce a new formula for their famous product. An American national institution had been tampered with – it was almost as bad as someone trying to alter the wording of the American Constitution! The American people were worried that the Real Thing wasn't quite the Real Thing any more. There is a thing called Real Christianity, but the problem is that the genuine article seems to get adulterated so much that there are many variations which are not quite Real. Usually this will happen gradually, over many years. That is what happened to the Jewish temple worship: it started off well, but it was progressively degraded by human sin and hypocrisy. The same thing happens in the church. The process is slow and subtle, but the end results can be devastating. Gradually things which are not compatible with Real Christianity begin to be accepted as part of Christian living, and in the end the church becomes seriously sick with corruption and very far removed from what God wants it to be.

Jesus wants us to embrace Real Christianity: he wants us to get rid of all hypocrisy, to be honest and pure, to be people who worship him in Spirit and in truth.

Chapter 7

THE NEW BIRTH

Now there was a man of the Pharisees named Nicodemus, a member of the Jewish ruling council. He came to Jesus at night and said, 'Rabbi, we know you are a teacher who has come from God. For no-one could perform the miraculous signs you are doing if God were not with him.'

In reply Jesus declared, 'I tell you the truth, no-one can see the kingdom of God unless he is born again.'

'How can a man be born when he is old?' Nicodemus asked. 'Surely he cannot enter a second time into his mother's womb to be born!'

Jesus answered, 'I tell you the truth, no-one can enter the kingdom of God unless he is born of water and the Spirit. Flesh gives birth to flesh, but the Spirit gives birth to spirit. You should not be surprised at my saying, "You must be born again."'

(John 3:1–3)

Here in this passage we see a pattern which crops up throughout John's Gospel. Someone asks Jesus a fairly straightforward question or makes a seemingly reasonable statement, and in response Jesus says something outrageous which completely bamboozles them! Time and again we see Jesus saying unlikely or enigmatic things which trigger people's imaginations and arouse their interest and help them to think through for themselves the issues he is raising. In this passage Nicodemus correctly says that the miraculous signs which Jesus is doing prove that his ministry has the stamp of God's authority upon it, and yet Jesus replies with something which at first glance seems to have no connection with what Nicodemus has said: Jesus tells him he must be born again.

A little further on in this chapter we have what is very probably the best-known verse in the whole of the New Testament:

For God so loved the world that he gave his one and only Son, that whoever believes in him shall not perish but have eternal life.

(John 3:16)

And then the last verse in the chapter is a summary of the whole of it:

Whoever believes in the Son has eternal life, but whoever rejects the Son will not see life, for God's wrath remains on him.

John chapter 3 leaves us in no doubt that we must be born again.

One day a man came to speak to George Whitefield, the great eighteenth-century evangelist, and said to him, 'Why on earth do you keep on saying in your sermons that I must be born again?' Whitefield looked him in the eye, pointed his finger at him and said, 'Because you *must* be born again.' This has been the message of all the great evangelists in history, from the Acts of the Apostles to George Whitefield and John Wesley to the mass evangelists of this century, like Billy Graham: they have called nation after nation to be born again, to make a completely clean breast of things, to begin again with God. That is not a new-fangled message which has been invented in America in recent years: it is a message which is as old as the New Testament itself.

We use a lot of different phrases these days to express this truth. We talk about being 'born again' or 'saved' or 'converted', about 'becoming a Christian' or 'getting a new life'. None of these phrases quite express the full truth of what it means to be a Christian, but all of them tell us a part of the truth. It is crucially important that we get the new birth – or, more accurately, that we *get Jesus* and so get born again in him.

An influential man

John 3:1 tells us that Nicodemus was one of the members of the Sanhedrin, the Jewish ruling council. What they said and decided was very important in Jewish society at that time. Prior to the Roman conquest of the region the Sanhedrin's word had literally been law: they had ruled the people. During the Roman occupation their power was more limited: very important decisions such as whether or not to execute a prisoner had to be referred to the Romans. However, in many other respects the Sanhedrin was still an important body. So Nicodemus was a member of the ruling elite of his nation: he was not some unintelligent nobody pestering Jesus with questions. He would have been a powerful, influential and affluent man. (We know he was wealthy because at the end of John's Gospel we read that he provided seventy-five pounds of myrrh and aloes for Jesus' burial.)

Verse 2 tells us that he came to see Jesus at night. Why was that? I think there were probably two reasons. First, Jewish rabbis (*i.e.* religious teachers) tended to do their teaching during the day, so that would have been as true of Jesus as much as any other rabbi. Jesus must have often been very busy. It seems that his days were not tightly planned, but because he was such a charismatic figure with such a magnetic personality people tended to flock to him, so most days he would have been busy teaching, healing the sick, casting out demons and so on. After the evening meal the Jews usually had a restful time until going to bed, so Nicodemus probably thought this would be a good opportunity to speak to Jesus without having to compete with anyone else for his attention.

However, there was also another reason why he came to Jesus at night, and that was his wish to keep it secret. He didn't want his fellow Sanhedrin members to know about it. By going at night he could sneak along the back-streets to the house where Jesus was staying and get there without being recognized. No-one would know that he had been to see Jesus. There would be no quizzical glances at the next Sanhedrin meeting; no whispers that Nicodemus had gone soft in the head in his old age and had drifted away from orthodox Judaism.

Why did he go to see Jesus? It must have been because he was dissatisfied with his religion. He doubt-less found it morally and intellectually demanding and rewarding in many respects, but in his heart of hearts he knew that there had to be something more. He would of course have been well acquainted with the Scriptures (what we call the Old Testament), and so he would have read the messianic prophecies. And so he was probably wondering if Jesus might be the Messiah, but he wasn't yet sure. So he came to Jesus and said, 'Jesus, what is your ministry all about? Who are you really? What are you doing here? What is your message? What does it mean to me personally?' It must have been a very important conversation to Nicodemus: it would have been a turning-point in his life. I believe that all that John gives us is selected snippets of that dialogue between Jesus and Nicodemus, probably as Jesus reported it to John at some later date.

What was it that drew Nicodemus to Jesus? First, he was drawn by the power of Jesus. Nicodemus said to him,

no-one could perform the miraculous signs you are doing if
God were not with him.

(verse 2)

So Nicodemus recognized God's authority being expressed in the amazing things Jesus was doing. When someone regularly heals the sick, casts demons out of people, makes the blind see and the deaf hear, you have to respond to it: you cannot simply say, 'That's interesting', and pass on by. The divine power which Jesus displayed compelled Nicodemus to take him seriously and to wonder who and what he was.

The Venerable Bede, one of England's earliest historians, tells a fascinating story about one of the Christian missionaries who evangelized the pagan Anglo-Saxons. The missionary came to a certain village and tried to explain the gospel message to its inhabitants. Their response was basically, 'That's very interesting, but we're quite happy with our pagan gods, thank you very much.' It became clear to the missionary that what was needed was a demonstration of God's almighty power, and so he asked, 'Is anyone in the village sick or blind?' There happened to be a middle-aged man who had been blind from birth. The missionary told him to kneel down and he laid his hands on the man's head and asked God to make him see. Immediately the man was able to see, for the first time in his life! Then the missionary explained the gospel to the people once again, and this time many were converted. What made the difference? They had seen a demonstration of God's power, and so they were then convinced by the missionary's preaching.

We see the same thing happening in the gospels. People witnessed the amazing power of Jesus over sickness and demons and even death itself, and so they asked questions about him. Who was this man? Could he be the promised Messiah? One of the terrible weaknesses of so much of our modern evangelism is that it is all words and no power. People hear a well presented gospel message, but because they don't actually see God's power at work, they don't feel compelled to believe the message. By contrast, in the gospels and also in the Acts of the Apostles we constantly see a demonstration of God's power and authority, and this always elicits a vigorous response from the people. Once the people had been humbled and amazed by God's power, Jesus and the apostles would then preach the good news to them and they would put their faith in Jesus. So that was one of the reasons why Nicodemus came to speak to Jesus: he had seen his wonderful power at work, and so he wanted to know more about this power and more about the person wielding it.

The second thing which drew Nicodemus to Jesus was his desire to know the truth. There were a lot of questions he wanted to ask Jesus: 'Who are you really? Are you the Messiah?' and so on. Many people are like that before they become Christians: their minds are full of questions, and they sense that only Jesus can give them satisfying answers. There is something missing from their lives and they want it badly. That something is the new birth, a relationship with the living God through Jesus.

What does 'born again' really mean?

The English language is always changing: new words are constantly being invented, some words are dropping out of usage, and other words take on new meanings. For example, consider what has happened to the word 'gay'. Originally it meant 'happy, merry, festive' and so forth. Thirty years ago, if you had said that you had gone to a gay party last night, people would have understood that you had had an enjoyable time. If you said the same thing today, people would conclude that you were a homosexual!

Something similar has happened to the term 'born again'. It is a biblical phrase, but unfortunately it has become part of normal English usage, and so its original meaning has been twisted so much that it is very hard to use it without being misunderstood. In most people's minds 'born again' means some kind of super-Christian: if you say you are a born-again Christian, people will think you are slightly fanatical. Manufacturers have used the term to sell their products: in a poster campaign a few years ago the Volkswagen car company described one of their new models as the 'born again Golf'. However, we should not let ourselves be robbed of the phrase 'born again'. It is a descriptive, biblical term, and we need to understand what it means because it expresses a vitally important truth.

Becoming a Christian is like being born all over again. Being born is a major event in anyone's life! We grow for nine months in the warmth and security of our mother's womb and then, within the space of just a few hours, we enter the world and we start our lives, no longer physically attached to mother. And for the mother giving birth is certainly no small matter! It's not something she does in between TV programmes, like popping down to the corner shop to buy a loaf of bread. It's something she has been preparing for for months, and she must make a great effort and endure a lot of pain in order to give birth to the child she has been carrying. Sometimes people speak of becoming a Christian as if it is a minor alteration in their lives. This is completely wrong: the new birth is a major, radical life-change – a total reorientation. We should not let the concept be debased: we should not talk about it in a light, superficial way.

Jesus said to Nicodemus that

. . . *no-one can enter the kingdom of God unless he is born of water and the Spirit.*

(John 3:5)

Some commentators think the reference to water means baptism in water, as in John chapter 1. However, I believe that this verse instead refers to natural, physical birth, because of what Jesus says in the next verse:

Flesh gives birth to flesh, but the Spirit gives birth to spirit.

Jesus is saying here that all of us need to be born physically (*Flesh gives birth to flesh*) and reborn spiritually (*the Spirit gives birth to spirit*). Physical birth is a radical new beginning, and so is spiritual birth.

Of course, not all Christians experience an explosive, cataclysmic transformation when they are born again. Their rebirth may take place over a long period of time, and they may not be able to remember clearly when it actually happened. This is particularly true of people who have grown up in Christian homes and have gone to church all their lives. As far as I know I became a Christian when I was about six years of age. Now, of course, it's not possible to commit a lot of serious sins before the age of six! However, in my childish way I was rebellious and bad-tempered; I was as naughty as most six-year-olds. Children are born as sinners: the idea that they are born perfect and pure and innocent is inaccurate. Anyone who has looked after a one-year-old child will tell you that he or she has a natural, inborn ability to be naughty! So I never experienced a clear-cut turning-point which I can definitely say was the time when I was converted. Rather, my simple, childlike commitment to Jesus grew and developed over the years into an adult faith in him.

There are a great many other Christians who have a similar story to tell. What matters is not whether or when we experienced a massive explosion of faith which we can clearly call our conversion, but whether our faith in Jesus has made a radical difference to our lives. If someone is converted from a thoroughly pagan background, some dramatic changes will take place in their life: that is inevitable if their conversion to Christ is real. The entire orientation of their lives will be radically altered. It is inconceivable that the difference would be unnoticeable to themselves and to other people. If, on the other hand, we grow up in a church background, we will probably not experience such a dramatic and rapid transformation. But what matters is, do we know and love and serve the Lord Jesus *now*? Never mind what happened when we were six or ten or sixteen. What God did in our past was wonderful and good, but are our lives now radically different from what they would have been if we had not been following Jesus all these years? Does our Christian faith make a difference to the way we live today? Do our lives express the fruit of the Spirit? When people get to know us, do they find themselves coming into contact with the living Christ, because he is living within us and expressing his life through us? If we are scarcely any different from the pagans around us, then there are grounds for questioning the reality of our 'conversion', whenever it is supposed to have happened.

By faith alone

We can only be born again by faith. Jesus says,

For God so loved the world that he gave his one and only Son, that whoever believes in him shall not perish but have eternal life.

(John 3:16)

We can never earn the right to be born again: the new birth is a gift from God, which he gives to those who believe in Jesus Christ.

Unfortunately the idea that we can earn salvation has infected the church at every level in every age. Many people think they can be saved by doing good works. Even if they come to understand the gospel and realize that only faith in Jesus can save them, and they become born again, they will often still try to earn God's approval by good works. They return to the old pattern of thinking, even though they know that salvation is by faith in Christ alone. This is all a tragic mistake. We can never make ourselves good enough for God: only Jesus can make us good enough. All we need to do is have faith in Jesus: we need to receive by faith the salvation and righteousness which God has provided for us in Jesus. The whole initiative of salvation is with God: he made the first move. It was not the case that humanity asked God for help, and in response he sent Jesus. No, the plan was God's: because he loved us he sent us his Son so that we could have eternal life in him.

Eternal life is referred to in verses 15, 16 and 36 of John chapter 3. What does this term mean? It does not mean just going to heaven when we die physically: it includes that, but it means more than that. Eternal life is living in the presence of God in joy and glory and freedom for all eternity. That will be our experience after our bodies die, but it is also our experience in the here and now once we have been born again. If we believe in Jesus as our Saviour, eternal life is ours right now – it is a gift from God which he gives us straight away. Jesus said,

I have come that they may have life, and have it to the full.
(John 10:10)

Jesus was talking about eternal life, which is life in all its fullness. Eternal life is human life as God intended it to be: joyful, vital, dynamic, beautiful, holy and lived in his presence. We begin to live this eternal life when we become Christians, and over the years it progressively transforms us so that increasingly we become fit to live in God's presence for ever.

In verses 3, 5 and 11 of John chapter 3 Jesus prefaces what he is about to say with the words, *I tell you the truth* ... In other words, he is saying, 'I am going to tell you the truth, Nicodemus. It's vitally important, so you had better take notice of what I am about to say.' Jesus was telling Nicodemus that he couldn't go away from that conversation thinking, 'Well, all those things Jesus said about being born again were very interesting. I must add them to my collection of clever things to say in intellectual discussions with my fellow scholars.' Jesus was telling him that the new birth was essential for him and that it should transform his life and behaviour. And Jesus is still saying the same thing to us today: 'This is the truth – it really matters what you do in response to my challenge to be born again. You are either born again or you are not; you must decide.'

The new birth in Jesus is not an optional extra for a super-spiritual few; we all need it. It is as vital to us as water or air. We would not live for more than a few minutes without air, and we cannot have eternal life without being born again. But because we are so spiritually blind and deaf we think we can go on ignoring the truth about new birth for years and years, assuming that everything is all right.

What do I do next?

Making that first commitment to Jesus is, of course, just the first step in the Christian life. We need to do more than take one step; we need to walk with Jesus for the rest of our lives. Having made a commitment to Jesus, what should we do next? Here is a checklist of things which recently converted people need to do:

1. Tell someone about it. The apostle Paul wrote,

... if you confess with your mouth, 'Jesus is Lord,' and believe in your heart that God raised him from the dead, you will be saved.

(Romans 10:9)

In other words, once we have committed our lives to Jesus we need to share what has happened to us with someone else. When they are converted many people remain secret disciples, and they don't tell anyone about it for weeks or months. This is unhelpful, because newly born Christians need support from mature Christians. If they don't get it they tend not to grow as quickly as they should.

2. Get baptized. Another important thing to do after you have been converted is to get baptized in water publicly. The Bible tells us that this is part and parcel of the new-birth experience.

3. Read your Bible and pray regularly. It is impossible to grow spiritually without feeding on God's Word and learning how to talk to God in prayer. It is very helpful to join a small group of Christians who read the Bible and pray together.

4. Join a local church. When you become a Christian you become a member of the body of Christ, which is the church. To grow you need to join a particular fellowship of local Christians.

These are the things which will ensure that a young Christian grows steadily. Those of us who have been Christians for some time need to have a pastoral concern for new Christians, helping and supporting them in any way we can. If they are converted as adults, we should be aware that they have radically to reorient their lives, and that isn't easy to do. Everything is turned on its head for them: their attitudes to their spouses, their children, their work, their possessions and their social life all have to change. This does not happen instantly; it will take months or even years for all these things to be worked through, and while this process of transformation is going on they will need support and encouragement from more mature Christians.

Nicodemus came to Jesus to discover the truth about him, and Jesus revealed to him the need to be born again spiritually. He was a seeker after the truth about Jesus, and he found that truth. All of us need to be born again, and yet we all need to continue being like Nicodemus: we all need to keep on discovering more truth, more spiritual maturity, from Jesus. We all need to go on getting to know Jesus better and experiencing more of his love and power in our lives. Just as people grow more mature physically, so too we need to mature spiritually; we need to go on discovering new depths in what it means to be born again in Jesus.

Chapter 8

MARKS OF MATURITY

... Jesus and his disciples went into the Judean countryside, where he spent some time with them, and baptised ... An argument developed between some of John's disciples and a certain Jew over the matter of ceremonial washing. They came to John and said to him, 'Rabbi, that man who was with you on the other side of the Jordan—the one you testified about—well, he is baptising, and everyone is going to him.'

To this John replied, 'A man can receive only what is given him from heaven. You yourselves can testify that I said, "I am not the Christ but am sent ahead of him." The bride belongs to the bridegroom. The friend who attends the bridegroom waits and listens for him, and is full of joy when he hears the bridegroom's voice. That joy is mine, and it is now complete. He must become greater; I must become less.'

(John 3:22–30)

When he first started preaching John the Baptist had made a huge impact on Judean society. He was a completely new phenomenon on the preaching circuit: there had not been anyone like him for generations – since the time of the Old Testament prophets. The crowds flocked to hear him preach. He was something of an odd-ball: he ate locusts and wild honey and wore clothes made of camel's hair (see Mark chapter 1). He baptized people in the River Jordan as a symbol of repentance from their sins, of turning from a sinful life to a life of righteousness and obedience to God. John was a sensation!

But here in the second half of John chapter 3 we see that John the Baptist's popularity was apparently waning: some of his disciples told him that Jesus was now also baptizing people *and everyone is going to him.* Increasingly Jesus was now the centre of everyone's attention and John the Baptist became a figure on the sidelines. John's mature response to this development is an example to everyone who is involved in Christian leadership and ministry.

He was spiritually mature enough to know that his ministry had reached its pinnacle and from now on would be of less significance. He knew it was time to move out of the limelight and to allow Jesus to come on to centre stage. He wanted Jesus, the Son of God, to have all the glory, and so when the time was right he was prepared to step back and let Jesus step forward. As he explained to his disciples (verses 28–29), he was not the Christ, but only the one sent ahead of him. John was just a signpost pointing to Jesus. He was merely the best man at the wedding, while Jesus was the bridegroom, to whom the bride (that is, the church) belonged.

Don't be jealous

There are three elements of John's maturity which we should note. First, he displayed an amazing lack of jealousy. Jesus was now getting all the people's attention, but John knew that that was the way God wanted it, and so he said to his disciples,

A man can receive only what is given him from heaven.

(verse 27)

God wanted him to be without a shred of jealousy about Jesus' ministry.

As I have travelled around the country meeting all sorts of Christians over the years, I have found that in the church there is a great deal of jealousy about other people's ministries. There is a tendency to run down other people's churches or denominations, other speakers, other organizations, people in other doctrinal camps – and the reason for this is quite simply that we want the glory and the credit and the attention all for ourselves. This is true on the level of the national church, and it is also true within local churches. Often there is jealousy about someone else's ministry in the church, particularly if theirs is similar to ours and they happen to be more gifted than we are!

Admit your limitations

John's second mark of maturity was his recognition of his own weaknesses. He said,

The one who comes from above [i.e. Jesus] is above all; the one who comes from the earth [i.e. John himself] belongs to the earth, and speaks as one from the earth.

(verse 31)

He was saying, 'Compared with Jesus, my ministry is as nothing. This man came from heaven and so can speak of heavenly things. I am from the earth and so can speak only of earthly things. Jesus is the Son of God – he is unique. He is the Lamb of God. I am merely his servant – all I have done is to point to him.'

John recognized that his ministry was limited, that he didn't have all the answers – and he pointed to the one who did have all the answers. Unfortunately many Christian leaders and counsellors today seem to think they do have all the answers. People come to them for help, and they think they can sort it all out by their own cleverness and giftedness. Instead they should be pointing the people to Jesus, who is the only one who always has all the answers. A counsellor who does not recognize his or her own weaknesses and limitations is dangerous. Jesus in describing this gave us a vivid picture:

If a blind man leads a blind man, both will fall into a pit.

(Matthew 15:14)

The proud counsellor is like a blind person leading another blind person off the edge of a precipice: they will both end up being injured, especially the person who came for help. Counsellors need to have John the Baptist's attitude: 'I am earthbound and so I don't have all the answers, but let me point you to Jesus, who knows everything.'

Give the glory to Jesus

The third aspect of John's maturity is his willingness to pass the glory on to Jesus. He told his disciples,

He must become greater; I must become less.

(verse 30)

He knew that more and more people were going to follow Jesus, and he would be left with almost no-one; he knew that he was meant to fade into the background while Jesus came increasingly into the foreground of the picture. And he accepted all this, because he was obedient to God.

Again, Christians today need to have John's attitude: we need to be men and women who are constantly passing the glory on to God. In any local church, a large part of the relationship problems are the result of spiritual immaturity. People are constantly trying to grab for themselves the glory which rightly belongs to God: they are desperate to be somebody, to be recognized, liked, appreciated, thanked and praised.

We may be praised for having done a job well in our

church fellowship, and then we may bask in that praise for a while, but then we bask in it for too long and we start to think that the project we were involved in was a success because of our own cleverness and efforts. Or our church as a whole may be doing very well: the membership may be increasing rapidly, the home groups may be bursting at the seams, new people are being brought into the leadership team all the time to cope with the increasing workload, people are being converted, touched by the Spirit, healed and delivered from bondage left, right and centre. If this is the case, then praise God for it! But what we often tend to do in situations of success like this is to start praising ourselves and our church: 'Come to our church! It's the place to be – we're a really dynamic bunch of Christians! You'll be impressed by us!' We actually start to believe that somehow we ourselves have accomplished all this, and God has merely helped us.

We must avoid this slippery slope: we must give the glory to God, because the Bible tells us that he will not share his glory with anyone else (Isaiah 42:8). If we try to hog some of the glory for ourselves we are being idolatrous, because we are not giving God the glory due to his name. We must recognize that any success we enjoy in our ministries is in reality God's success: he has accomplished it, his power has made it possible, his authority has made it happen. In other words, we need to be humble before God, remembering that we are just his creatures and he is the almighty Creator.

There is an old hymn which expresses this very well. The first verse ends, 'All of self, and none of Thee' – that's the proud attitude we start with. The second verse ends, 'Some of self, and some of Thee' – now we are becoming a little more mature as Christians. The third verse ends, 'Less of self, and more of Thee' – we are making real progress in maturity, but we still have some way to go. The final verse says, 'None of self, and all of Thee' – at last we have got to the state of mind God wants us to have. This was the spiritual state at which John the Baptist had arrived. He was so certain of his place with God that he didn't need the applause of the crowd any more. I think that is a very good definition of true spiritual maturity: when we don't need that constant patting on the back, when we don't need to be told how wonderful we are, when our ego doesn't need regular stroking. We are so secure in God that we really want all the praise and glory to go to him.

Chapter 9

BREAKING DOWN BARRIERS

Now [Jesus] had to go through Samaria, so he came to a town in Samaria called Sychar, near the plot of ground Jacob had given to his son Joseph. Jacob's well was there, and Jesus, tired as he was from the journey, sat down by the well ...

When a Samaritan woman came to draw water, Jesus said to her, 'Will you give me a drink?' (His disciples had gone into the town to buy food.) The Samaritan woman said to him, 'You are a Jew and I am a Samaritan woman. How can you ask me for a drink?' (For Jews do not associate with Samaritans.)

(John 4: 4–9)

Racial prejudice

In order to understand this passage we need to know a little about the history of the area. Samaria was the northern part of the Roman province of Judea, located to the north of Jerusalem and to the south of Galilee. The inhabitants of southern Judea and Galilee were Jews, but the people of Samaria were a mixed race. Centuries before Samaria had been peopled by Jews, but when the Assyrians had conquered the area they had deported most of the Jews to other parts of their empire, leaving just a few behind. Then they had settled people of other nations in Samaria, and eventually the Jewish remnant had intermarried with them, and the Samaritan nation was the result.

Consequently the pure-blooded Jews of Jesus' time saw the Samaritans as the lowest of the low, since in their eyes interbreeding with Gentiles was the unforgivable sin. To the Jews, the Samaritans were half-breeds, outcasts, the dregs of humanity. In the Jewish scheme of things Jewish men were the superior caste, with Jewish women as a lower order, the Gentiles lower still and the Samaritans even worse than the Gentiles.

Because of this history of racial prejudice the Samaritan woman at the well was amazed that Jesus should speak to her, let alone ask her for a drink of water. By doing so Jesus was taking the social conventions of his day and tearing them apart. Effectively he was saying to the woman, 'I don't care about your racial extraction; you were made in the image of God, and so you are worthy of respect as a person. I will not tolerate an unnatural distinction between God's children. I reject this Jew–Samaritan animosity which has been festering for generations. It is unimportant. What matters is the fact that I am God's Son and so I have something to share with you. I am going to talk to you about me and my love.'

Breaking down artificial social barriers which separated people was one of the hallmarks of Jesus' ministry. The ancient world was rife with racial hatred and prejudice. The Jews thought that because they were God's chosen people they were better than anyone else; the Greeks thought that their brilliant civilization made them a superior breed, all other peoples being barbarians by comparison; the Romans thought that because they had conquered the whole of the Mediterranean world they were the master race. Jesus was the very first person to boldly and clearly affirm by his life and his words that racial distinctions did not matter, because everyone was equal in the eyes of God.

We Christians need to affirm today that the Jesus who

hated racial prejudice back in the first century still hates racism today. We need to say this very clearly, because, sadly, throughout history the Christian church has often been guilty of racial prejudice. Only a few generations ago some Christian preachers were publicly saying that black people had been created by God as sub-human, or at least inferior to white people, and consequently it was legitimate to enslave blacks and take over their countries by force. In this nation a great many Christians have shared our society's basic assumption that because we are white and British we are better than other peoples, and there are still many Christians today who have such an attitude, even if only subconsciously.

Now, of course, there is nothing wrong with being proud of our country. There are many fine things in our British national life and history. However, that does not mean it is right to have a nationalistic, jingoistic attitude which says that we are the cream of the world and everyone else is second-rate. We modern Christians need to be aware of the racial prejudice of the church in the past.

We need to understand clearly and say clearly that racism is a sin. All people are made in the image of God, and all people are sinners in need of Jesus as their Saviour. There is only one distinction between people that matters, and that is the one between those sinners who have been saved and those sinners who have not. And those who are saved are not permitted to feel superior about it; they are saved only by God's grace, and their task is to encourage other people to respond to Christ.

Had Jesus been like his fellow Jews he would never have spoken to the Samaritan woman: he would have assumed that God was not interested in her. We need to be careful that we do not make that kind of assumption about people, for whatever reason. To God, no-one is beyond the pale. We very easily fall into

77

the trap of thinking that certain groups of people are beyond the reach of God's love. They may be certain racial or ethnic groups, or people of different religions, or people of a different social class. Subconsciously we think things like, 'Surely those dreadful people with purple spiky hair and brass studs in their ears and noses wouldn't ever respond to the gospel message', or 'Those people swear and get drunk a lot – there's no way they're ever going to want to hear about God's love', or 'Those people are so well off and comfortable and smug and self-satisfied that they have no idea that they need God, so what's the point of telling them about Jesus?'

We may think that surely there can't be any racial or social prejudice in our church – we're all nice Christians, so there's no way we could be guilty of anything as unpleasant as that. But examine your own heart: is it completely free of prejudice? I doubt it. And if there is prejudice in our own hearts, there is sure to be prejudice in the hearts of many others in our church. Prejudice has no place in the Christian life; it is a denial of Jesus' love for all people. Let's get rid of it!

Sexual prejudice

The fact that Jesus spoke to a Samaritan at the well shows that he had no time for racial prejudice; the fact that he spoke to a Samaritan *woman* shows that he had no time for sexual prejudice either. We can see a hint of the sexism of Jewish society at that time in verse 27:

Just then the disciples returned and were surprised to find [Jesus] talking with a woman.

Talking with a strange woman was not something which Jewish men usually did, and talking to a *Samaritan* woman would have been doubly unthinkable!

In Jewish culture at that time women were very much

second-class citizens. They were thought to be an unwelcome distraction to any God-fearing man who wanted to obey the Law. Among the Pharisees there was a group whose Hebrew name meant 'the bruised and bleeding ones'. They acquired this strange name because it was their rule to shut their eyes whenever they saw a woman, so as not to be distracted from the observance of the Law. As a result they would often walk into things accidentally and injure themselves! There was a tremendous prejudice at the heart of Judaism against the female half of the human race.

The apostle Paul is often said to have been prejudiced against women. The opposite is true, in fact. It was Paul who wrote,

There is neither Jew nor Greek, slave nor free, male nor female, for you are all one in Christ Jesus.

(Galatians 3:28)

Peter too was quite a revolutionary in this respect. Part of their ministry was to rescue the Jews and the whole of the culture of their time from its rank sexual prejudice. It was part of their message that the ground at the foot of the cross is level ground, and everyone is on an equal footing there – black and white, Jew and Gentile, male and female. Now, of course, the fact that men and women are equal in God's sight does not mean that they are *the same*. Men and women are different, and may have different roles to play in the church.

Chapter 10

JESUS' METHOD OF EVANGELISM

Jesus answered her, 'If you knew the gift of God and who it is that asks you for a drink, you would have asked him and he would have given you living water.'

'Sir,' the woman said, 'you have nothing to draw with and the well is deep. Where can you get this living water? ...'

Jesus answered, 'Everyone who drinks this water will be thirsty again, but whoever drinks the water I give him will never thirst. Indeed, the water I give him will become in him a spring of water welling up to eternal life.'

The woman said to him, 'Sir, give me this water so that I won't get thirsty and have to keep coming here to draw water.'

(John 4:10–15)

A positive offer

There are some very valuable lessons for us in the way in which Jesus talked to this woman and brought her to faith in himself. He said to her,

Everyone who drinks this water [i.e. the water from the well] will be thirsty again, but whoever drinks the water I give him will never thirst. Indeed, the water I give him will become in him a spring of water welling up to eternal life.

(John 4:13–14)

The first part of his evangelistic technique was to make

81

her a positive and attractive offer. He didn't say, 'Lady, I've got something to tell you: unless you believe in me you'll be condemned.' Rather, he said, 'If you drink the living water which I have to offer, you will have in your life a well which will spring up inside you and will never, never run dry.'

We don't know much about this woman, but we do know that she was inquisitive and questioning. She carried on this conversation with Jesus – she didn't just walk off. So she was interested by what Jesus said about the spring of water which he had to offer. He was saying to her, 'Your life need not remain as sad and empty as it is now. Instead you can have joy and love and real, abundant life.'

Of course, when we witness to people it's right that they should be told the consequences of rejecting Jesus: they should know that without him they will face eternal death rather than eternal life. But that should not be the main thrust of our witnessing; at the forefront of our message should be the fact that in Jesus we can have a well of living water within us.

Sadly, many Christians have not really experienced very much of this living water. Why is this? Because a well runs dry if no water is drawn from it. If we are Christians we have this well of living water within us, but it will only keep springing up if we draw water from it. Many Christians don't keep on drawing the water out. They know there is a spring of water in their lives, but they just admire it – they don't go and drink from it, letting it spring up and fill them with life and joy. As a result, when they talk to others about the Christian faith and how wonderful it is, their lives contradict what they are saying. They may say that coming to know Jesus is the most wonderful thing that ever happened to them, but the people they are witnessing to wonder why they look so miserable if being a Christian is supposed to be so marvellous. To use an analogy, sometimes mothers may ask their families at the meal-table if they are enjoying their dinners, and the family are too kind or polite to say that it's horrible! They say, 'Yes, it's lovely, Mum,' but the expressions on their faces say something else! So in evangelism we need to make people the positive offer which Jesus made, but in order for that offer to be credible we first have to experience the reality of it for ourselves.

Repentance

The second element of Jesus' evangelistic approach is to lead the woman to repentance. He says to her,

You are right when you say you have no husband. The fact is, you have had five husbands, and the man you now have is not your husband.

(verses 17–18)

He gently but firmly reminds her of her own sin. Once we have made people the positive offer, we have to lead them to repentance. It is sadly the case that many people today make an initial commitment to Jesus, having heard the positive offer about eternal life in him, and yet after a few weeks or months they drift away from Christian commitment. Why is this? Usually it is because they have not been led to repentance: they have not been shown that they need to be sorry in God's presence for the sin in their lives. They have been offered salvation too lightly, too easily: they are told in effect, 'Just come to Jesus and everything will be okay.' That is true in a sense, but unless there is conviction of sin, unless there is repentance and a turning away from the dirt of the old life, the person's conversion will be unreal and superficial. It certainly won't be what the New Testament means by conversion. Jesus knew that the woman at the well needed to be confronted by the fact that she had been leading an immoral lifestyle. For her conversion to be real she had to recognize her sinfulness and turn away from it.

A red herring

Now comes the third stage of the evangelistic process. After Jesus has convicted her of her sin she attempts to steer the conversation in another direction by throwing in a red herring:

Our fathers worshipped on this mountain [Mount Gerizim], but you Jews claim that the place where we must worship is in Jerusalem.

(verse 20)

Jesus was getting personal, and so she tried to make him talk about something else.

If you have ever done any evangelism, you must have encountered some red herrings like this. As soon as you challenge people with the fact that they need to repent of their sins, they will throw in an intellectual question, such as 'Why is there so much suffering in the world?' or 'Why are there so many different Christian denominations?' or 'Why has there been so much hypocrisy in the church down the ages?' These are all perfectly legitimate questions, but the people may be asking them not because they want answers but simply to divert the conversation away from the uncomfortable subject of their own sin. (Also, of course, some of the red herrings one encounters in evangelism are just plain silly, such as 'Did Adam have a navel or not?' – the issue being that he couldn't have had a navel, since he didn't have a mother, but then if he didn't have a mother, was he a proper human being like the rest of us? …)

The worst thing we can do in situations like these is to try to answer the question: we will inevitably get bogged down. The answer doesn't matter, since the person doesn't really want one anyway. Of course, if the person is asking a genuine question out of honest curiosity, it's a different matter. If we are able to answer the question, all well and good, but if not, we can say, 'I don't know the answer to that question, but I'll try to find out for you. But getting back to what I said earlier about the need for repentance ...'

We should take note of the way Jesus deals with the woman's red herring. He answers it very briefly, saying that the place of worship does not really matter and telling her that

a time is coming ... when true worshippers will worship the Father in spirit and truth, for they are the kind of worshippers the Father seeks.

(verses 21–23)

And then he gets right down to the fact that he is the Messiah: *I who speak to you am he'* (verse 26). He doesn't waste time on this question, but tells the woman what she really needs to know for her salvation.

Conversion and witnessing

So the fourth stage in this evangelistic dialogue is that the woman comes to realize that Jesus is the Messiah. Gently and simply her eyes have been opened, and she sees that this is no ordinary man: this is the Christ, the Messiah, the Anointed One sent from God, and he loves her. The same is still true today: once people have got past the red herring stage they need to know that Jesus wants to touch them and give them new life.

After that comes the fifth and final stage of this story: the woman goes and tells other people about Jesus, about the wonderful discovery she has made:

Many of the Samaritans from that town believed in him because of the woman's testimony, 'He told me everything I ever did'.

(verse 39)

Having been evangelized herself, the woman believes and goes to evangelize other people, and so the process becomes a circle. Just as God has a reproductive plan for the human race, in which a man and a woman are united sexually and produce children, so God also has a reproductive plan for the church, and it is expressed in the five steps we have been thinking about.

If every Christian worked and prayed to bring one person to Christ annually, every year all our churches would double in size. That sounds simple, so why doesn't it happen? I believe it is because we are so preoccupied with doing things which are good that we don't have time to do the things which are best – that is, winning people to Christ. The devil keeps us so busy with second-rate things that we miss the thing that really matters: getting people into the kingdom.

I believe we prefer mass evangelism (that is, big rallies, evangelistic services and so on) to personal evangelism (that is, telling people about Jesus ourselves) because in mass evangelism, if the results are disappointing, we cannot be personally blamed for it: there is no weight of responsibility upon us. We can criticize the way the evangelistic campaign was run with safety, and no-one can point the finger at us.

Perhaps bringing one person to Christ every year is an unrealistic goal; but if so, why? Why should it not be possible? If we did it, we might not need any other form of evangelism!

Signs and wonders

In our churches today we often think of signs and wonders and so forth as happening within church services and Christian meetings. It's very encouraging that prayer for healing is now a common thing and that in many churches there is a regular opportunity for people to be prayed for at the end of services. However, in the New Testament healings, signs and wonders and the demonstration of God's power are not primarily a part of the church's worship-life but are instead an integral part of *evangelism*.

We can see plenty of evidence of this just in the first four chapters of John's Gospel. In chapter 1 Jesus had a supernatural insight about Nathanael, seeing him sitting under the fig tree while he was still a long way off. This insight so impressed Nathanael that he believed in Jesus as the Messiah. In chapter 2 at the wedding in Cana Jesus turned the water into wine, and as a result his disciples believed in him. And in chapter 4 we have the case of the Samaritan woman at the well. Jesus chatted to her for a few minutes and shared with her a revelation about her past life. She thought, 'How could he know that I have had five husbands and the man I now have is not my husband? He must be a prophet!' And afterwards she believed that he was the Messiah. In each case we see Jesus acting in supernatural power, and this power gave divine authority to the words he said to the people. As a result of this combination of word and power they were converted. We see the same pattern of evangelism in the rest of the gospels, in the Acts of the Apostles and in the New Testament letters: God's power working with God's Word resulted in people being saved. *Jesus Christ is the same yesterday and today and for ever* (Hebrews 13:8), so if God worked in that way in New Testament times, he may want to work in the same way today.

It is essential that we do not lose sight of the real purpose of miracles: their purpose is to point people to Jesus. If we look at John chapter 4, we see that the woman brought the people to meet Jesus. They had heard her testimony about his amazing insight about her past life, so their curiosity had been stirred. But after he had spent two days with them, telling them the good news, they came to believe in him as the Messiah. They said to the woman,

We no longer believe just because of what you said; now we have heard for ourselves, and we know that this man really is the Saviour of the world.

(verse 42)

So they were no longer preoccupied by the miraculous; they had put their faith in Jesus as the Messiah. A miracle had initially drawn them to him, but once they had encountered him their attention was fixed on him rather than the miracle itself. The miracle had served to point them to Jesus.

The word which John's Gospel uses for 'miracle' is different from the words used in the other three gospels. Matthew, Mark and Luke use words such as *teras, exousia* and *dunamis,* which mean 'power' and 'authority'. John's Gospel uses the word *seimeion,* which means 'sign'. The miracles are 'signs' which point to Jesus.

So it is possible for our interest in miracles to become unhealthy; we can become excessively interested in the signs for their own sakes, rather than Jesus, the one to whom they are meant to point. We want miracles for us, but God gives miracles for the world, to convert people. The world is supposed to look at the miracles so that they can see beyond them to the Person who is doing them. We Christians are supposed to see beyond the miracles already; we are supposed to know Jesus well enough to love him for who he is and for what he has done for us by saving us. The trouble is, some Christians seem to suffer from arrested spiritual development: they are so immature that they have never quite got beyond the stage of being excited about the miracles for their own sake. Now, of course, when God works a miracle we should be excited about it, but we should be excited because *God* has done it, and that should lead us to praise and worship him and give him the glory for it. If we allow our thoughts to focus on the miracle without ever seeing beyond it to the Miracle-Maker, our attitude becomes idolatrous. Effectively we are saying that God's miracles are more exciting to us than God himself.

Jesus said some very strong words against the religious leaders of his day, who kept asking him, 'Give us a sign.' But his reply was 'No, there will be no sign other than the one given to Jonah: he was in the whale's belly for three days and then rose from death. The same thing is going to happen to me: I will be dead for three days and then I will be resurrected. I am not a mere entertainer who performs magic tricks for your amusement. I do miracles in order to show the world who I am – the Messiah' (see Luke 11:29–32 and Matthew 12:38–45). The church today needs to take that lesson to heart. Miracles and signs and wonders are not meant to boost our egos, so that we can say, 'Come to our church – it's really great! We're into signs and wonders!' The miraculous is given for the conversion of the world.

At the end of John chapter 4 we have an illustration of all this in the healing of the royal official's son. Just listen to the wistfulness in Jesus' voice:

Unless you people see miraculous signs and wonders, you will never believe.

(verse 48)

Jesus must have been tired of the people's lack of faith in him; all they wanted was miracles. And yet graciously he did as the official asked and said, *You may go. Your son will live.* The official might have argued with Jesus, badgering him to come with him and lay his healing hands on the boy. But Jesus told him to go, and he obeyed, trusting Jesus for the healing of his son: *The man took Jesus at his word and departed.*

Christians today need to be people who take Jesus at his word. When he tells us to preach his good news or pray for a miracle, we should obey; when he says, 'You may go', we should go, trusting him to do as he says he will do. Then we will see signs and wonders, not just in church on Sundays but out in the streets of our local communities. Jesus' power will be manifested out in the world, and people will be pointed towards him and will come to faith in him.

Chapter 11

THREE LESSONS TO LEARN

Some time later, Jesus went up to Jerusalem for a feast of the Jews. Now there is in Jerusalem near the Sheep Gate a pool, which in Aramaic is called Bethesda and which is surrounded by five covered colonnades. Here a great number of disabled people used to lie—the blind, the lame, the paralysed. One who was there had been an invalid for thirty-eight years. When Jesus saw him lying there and learned that he had been in this condition for a long time, he asked him, 'Do you want to get well?'

'Sir,' the invalid replied, 'I have no-one to help me into the pool when the water is stirred. While I am trying to get in, someone else goes down ahead of me.'

Then Jesus said to him, 'Get up! Pick up your mat and walk.' At once the man was cured; he picked up his mat and walked.

(John 5:1–9)

The first thing to note about this passage is the fact that it bears all the marks of historical authenticity. It describes the pool of Bethesda in some detail (much of which is supported by strong archaeological evidence). It was obviously a real place which anyone who knew Jerusalem would have been familiar with. Here John is writing about something he saw for himself in a real place in real history. So this account of the healing of

91

the lame man cannot be dismissed as fiction.

Another point to make is that there is in fact a little Jewish joke in these verses. Most Jewish humour is to do with plays on words, and that is the case here. In the original language here Jesus in effect said to the man, 'Your mat has been carrying you for all these years; now you carry your mat!'

The pool of Bethesda was a special place where sick people went in the hope of being healed miraculously by God. Today many people go to Lourdes in France for the same reason, and in some cases God does indeed heal them. But the wonderful thing is that because we are now in the new dispensation, God's miraculous power is no longer linked to particular places but rather to a Person – Jesus – and hence to the church, which is made up of all those people in whom the Spirit of Jesus dwells. Back in the Old Testament God's working in power was associated with particular places such as the Tabernacle and the Temple and Jerusalem, but ever since the cross, the resurrection and Pentecost, God's power has been expressed wherever Jesus is. And, of course, Jesus is everywhere, so today miracles can happen anywhere at all – in the street, in a church, in our homes. So we no longer need to go to a 'holy' place for healing – for us, anywhere can be the pool of Bethesda.

In the King James Version of the Bible there was an extra verse (verse 4) in this passage which is omitted by the NIV and the RSV. In the earliest and most reliable manuscripts of John's Gospel it does not appear, and it seems that it was added later as a word of explanation. The NIV gives verse 4 as a footnote:

From time to time an angel of the Lord would come down and stir up the waters. The first one into the pool after each such disturbance would be cured of whatever disease he had.

So that was what the Jews at the time believed. One can

imagine what it must have been like whenever the waters stirred: there would have been an unseemly rush to be the first into the water. The man who was healed by Jesus had been there for thirty-eight years and had never managed to be first in.

The name Bethesda literally means 'the house of mercy', and that is very fitting, for Jesus, the Son of God, came to the pool and showed God's mercy to the lame man. Here we see the difference between the old dispensation and the new vividly demonstrated. Under the old system, in which 'blessing' was located in certain places, the lame man had been disappointed for many years. But along came Jesus, the inaugurator of the new dispensation, and he was able to heal the man there and then, completely and instantly. We see that the new is infinitely superior to the old, for it is centred on Jesus, the Son of God.

A pastoral lesson

There are three lessons for us to learn from this story: a pastoral one, a practical one and a personal one. First, the pastoral lesson. Jesus asked the man, *Do you want to get well?* The man, thinking in terms of the old covenant, replied, 'But I can't get down into the pool in time, and so someone else always gets in first.' But Jesus was saying to him, 'You don't understand the question I am asking. I'm not asking if you want me to help you down into the pool. Never mind the pool – it doesn't matter any more. What I'm saying is, *Do you want to get well?* If you do, I have the power to make that happen right now.' Jesus told him to pick up his mat and walk, and so the man was transferred from the old covenant, with its dependence on holy places, to the new dispensation, with its dependence upon Jesus. Having been translated into a new spiritual dimension, the man walked off with his mat, made well at long last.

Jesus' question, *Do you want to get well?* is crucially important. He was saying to the man, 'Do you really want to be healed, or have you despaired, have you accepted your sickness, so that you are quite content to stay here by the pool for the rest of your life?' Jesus asks the same question of each of us today: Do we want to be well? In John's Gospel the word 'salvation' literally means 'wholeness'. We may not be physically sick, but do we want to be saved, whole, complete people in Christ? Do we really want to enter into the fullness of the new covenant in Jesus?

It has to be said that many of us do not really want to be well in this full sense. Many Christians secretly enjoy being sick; it gives them something to talk about, it makes them the centre of attention. They draw people's care and love towards them and they suck it into themselves as if they were vacuum cleaners. Some Christians are walking black holes: no matter how much love and care is poured into them, they will never get well because they don't really want to get well.

We all need to ask ourselves whether we really want to be whole, healed people, or are we content with being emotionally and spiritually sick and crippled? Are we in fact basically satisfied with the sort of people we are? Jesus comes to us and says, 'Do you want to get well? If you don't really want to be whole, then I can't help you.' Even the Son of God is unable to help us if we don't want his help.

Time and again I have been in pastoral situations in which it has become clear that the people concerned don't want a cure – they just want attention. Jesus is not in the business of giving people attention just for the sake of it; he is in the business of making people whole.

The same principle also applies to being filled with the Holy Spirit. A. W. Tozer writes, 'We are as full of the Holy Spirit as we want to be.' If we don't want him, we won't have him. We will only have the fullness of the Spirit if we really long for it and desire it.

Do we want to be well, or are we happy to sit by the pool of Bethesda for thirty-eight or more years, cherishing our weaknesses and using them to get attention? Do we want to get up and walk or are we content to crawl from one mistake to another, from one failure to another? I know these are hard words, but they are a challenge we all need to consider.

A practical lesson

The day on which this took place was a Sabbath.

(verse 9)

The Sabbath (our Saturday) was a very special day to the Jews. On that day people were supposed to refrain from all kinds of work. The Jews thought that to heal a lame man, as Jesus had done, was work.

So, because Jesus was doing things on the Sabbath, the Jews persecuted him.

(verse 16)

The Jews had all sorts of rules and regulations about the Sabbath: how far it was permissible to walk, for instance. And they had introduced a number of loopholes – for example, if you stopped off for a meal for more than an hour while you were out walking, you could cancel out the distance you had already walked and start again. Altogether there were 617 laws which they had to obey in order to be devout Jews, so it was all very complicated and convoluted.

Jesus took the rule about the Sabbath and turned it on its head. He said,

The Sabbath was made for man, not man for the Sabbath.

(Mark 2:27)

In other words, the priority was *God's* work, not man

refraining from work, not some man-made set of legalistic rules and regulations. Jesus has brought in a new covenant, and so the whole nature of the Sabbath has changed. Jesus cut across all the barriers and showed that the Sabbath was not made in order that people should be oppressed and made miserable by it; rather, the Sabbath was made for mankind so that we could be free to worship God without all the restrictions and pressures which the workaday world places on us.

Often Christians who have been brought up in a church background have a misunderstanding about the Sabbath. They have grown up in an environment in which Sunday was hedged about by rules and regulations and not by the Spirit. There were things we were allowed to do on Sundays and there were things we couldn't do because somehow it was a special sort of day. But if it is wrong to do something on a Sunday, it should also be wrong to do it on a Monday or any other day of the week. In a sense the days are equal in God's sight.

The point about Sunday is that it is the day of the resurrection. Jesus rose from the dead on a Sunday, so we keep Sunday as a special day, as our Sabbath. It is a day given over to worship and thinking about God. Rest is an important part of the Christian Sunday, but only part of it: primarily Sunday should be about celebrating the resurrection of Jesus. Part of that celebration may well be having a fun time with the kids playing football or flying a kite, but it is important that celebration is the central priority in our Sundays. So anything which diminishes our opportunity on a Sunday to go to church and worship God is wrong. Watching TV or going for a bike ride on a Sunday is not wrong in itself, but these activities would be wrong if they kept us away from church.

We need to be free to worship God in Spirit and in

truth on a Sunday, so we should be free from unhelpful distractions, but we should also be free from legalism. Sunday is not about compelling our children to sit still and be quiet and look holy all day. Sunday is not about banning our children and ourselves from doing anything even remotely enjoyable. It is not about repressing children's natural appetite for fun and enjoyment. It is not about locking all their books and comics and toys away and telling them they can't watch television either. If we take that attitude, it is hardly surprising that children grow up associating Sundays with boredom, and then they may come to regard the Christian faith itself as boring and may want to have nothing to do with it. If Sundays are dull for our children, we may well find that as they get older they make sure that they get involved in activities and pursuits which take them away from home on Sundays and make it impossible for them to come to church.

There has always been an element of hypocrisy in the traditional, legalistic Sunday. Oh yes, it was the day on which no-one was supposed to work, but who was it who was expected on Sundays to cook the best meal of the week for everyone and do all the washing-up afterwards, while the rest of the family sat around taking it easy? It was Mother, of course! Whole generations of Christian mothers never knew the meaning of the phrase 'day of rest'! Somehow it was permissible for Mother to work on a Sunday even though no-one else could work – that particular loophole was quite acceptable to those who just sat around all day!

Of course, this will all be Greek to those Christians who have come from non-church backgrounds; they will wonder what on earth all the fuss is about. Sundays have never been a problem for them. Well, praise God for that! Those Christians don't need to de-programme themselves from all the legalism that some of us grew up with.

A personal lesson

Finally we have the personal lesson which this passage teaches us. That lesson is this: that *Jesus is God*. Jesus said to the Jews,

'My Father is always at his work to this very day, and I, too, am working.' For this reason the Jews tried all the harder to kill him; not only was he breaking the Sabbath, but he was even calling God his own Father, making himself equal with God.
(John 5:17–18)

Jesus was clearly saying here that he was God. The Jesus who walked this earth, preached the gospel, healed the sick and raised the dead said that God was his Father and that he himself was God. The Scriptures leave us in no doubt about the fact that Jesus was fully God as well as fully human. He was the Son of God, the Second Person of the Holy Trinity. All the sects which say that Jesus was merely a good man and a great moral teacher are utterly wrong: he was indeed those things, but he was also God. John chapter 1 tells us that he was the divine Word who was with God in the beginning of all things; he was not a mere man.

Jesus is God – the Lord of Lords and the King of Kings. There have been some great kings and leaders in the history of the world: Nebuchadnezzar, the Pharaohs, Alexander the Great, Augustus, Constantine, Charlemagne, Louis XIV, Napoleon, the Russian tsars, the Chinese emperors, Queen Victoria, the American presidents … But all of them were miniscule Mickey Mouse figures compared with Jesus, the King of Kings. They are all dead, but he is alive today and lives forever. They were all mortal human beings, but he is the eternal God.

This is the personal lesson for us all: Jesus is God, and

we must respond personally to that truth. We must say to him, 'Yes, Jesus, we acknowledge that you are the Almighty God. We recognize who you are and we humbly worship you with all our hearts. We give you the praise that is due to you.'

Chapter 12

DO WHAT THE FATHER DOES

Jesus gave them this answer: 'I tell you the truth, the Son can do nothing by himself; he can only do what he sees his Father doing, because whatever the Father does the Son also does. For the Father loves the Son and shows him all he does ...'

(John 5:19–20)

One might have assumed that Jesus, the Son of God, the great teacher and healer, would have gone around Galilee and Judea doing his own thing, but these verses tell us that he never did his own thing; rather, he always did God's thing. He was so close to his Father that he always wanted to do what his Father wanted to do. That is evident throughout John's Gospel. Jesus is always shown as working in tandem with his Father.

That was true of the ministry of Jesus, and it should also be true in our own lives as Christians. We need to be committed to doing what God is doing. When we see God doing something, we should get on and do it with him. I have to admit that when I was younger I quite often used to struggle on with projects and endeavours for a long time, and finally I would begin to wonder, 'Is God in this? Does God want me to be doing this?' And often the reason why things weren't going very well was that indeed God did not want me to do the thing I had been doing. It might be a worthwhile thing in principle, but it was not what God wanted me to be doing at that particular time. There are times in our lives and in the life of a church when we have to assess a situation and ask if God is working in it any more. If he is not, then we need to move on to something else – to the thing that he *is* doing. These days, having learned a little from those past experiences, when I am asked to get involved in a certain project or activity, I pray, 'God, are you really in this? Is this thing what you are doing? If it is, I want to be involved in it, but if it isn't, I don't want anything to do with it. I only want to do what you really want me to do.'

Sometimes people stay in local churches which are as dead as doornails for years longer than God wants them to. God is not really working in that church any more. The people never ask God, 'Are you working here? Do you want me to stay here or do you want me to move on?' Across the doors of some of these churches you could write the Hebrew word 'Ichabod', meaning 'the glory has departed': God has gone, he is not there any more, he has left that fellowship. And yet people stay in that church and their own spiritual lives become drier and drier and encrusted and bitter and twisted, and eventually almost dead. Now, of course, in some cases God may well want people to stay in such a dry, dead church for years in order to be a witness for him there. But we need to make sure that this is the case: we should not just assume that God wants us to stay in a situation simply because we have already been there a long time.

I know that what I have just written may sound unkind, but it needs to be said. Of course, we should not be judging and condemning about churches and organizations which are dying spiritually: we should not think that we are better than the Christians who belong to them. Whatever life and blessing our churches enjoy is all a gift from God, not the result of our own cleverness or righteousness. However, there is little point in masking the truth: if God is no longer working in a situation it is clearly time for us to get out and go where he is working. We must do only the things which God is doing. If we work with God, then we can be sure that the results will be encouraging, because God is truly in that situation.

Jesus the Judge

Jesus told the Jews,

… the Father judges no-one, but has entrusted all judgment to the Son, that all may honour the Son just as they honour the Father.

(John 5:22–23)

God has given the responsibility for judging the world to Jesus. Every person who has ever lived – men, women and children of all eras, nations, religions, races and social classes – will one day stand before Jesus to be judged by him. On that day he will want to know one thing: do we know him as Lord and Saviour? If we do not, no matter what sort of person we have been, we will be pronounced guilty. We may have been a good, kind, considerate person; we may have been a good husband or wife, a good father or mother, a good citizen, a good church member; we may have been dedicated to a worthy, socially useful career; we may have done a lot of work for charity … None of that will be of any consequence. All Jesus will want to know is, 'Did you accept me as your Saviour?' We have a very simple choice: either to accept him as Saviour now, while it is not too late, or to face him as Judge on the last day.

Discover a Person, not a book

Jesus said to the Jews,

You diligently study the Scriptures because you think that by them you possess eternal life. These are the Scriptures that testify about me, yet you refuse to come to me to have life.

(John 5:39–40)

The Bible is the Word of God; it is a wonderful book, but it is not Jesus. The Bible points to Jesus: when we read it we are meant to expect to meet Jesus, not simply to learn a lot of facts about biblical history.

Those of us who grew up in a church background will have gone to Sunday School, and there we will have learnt a lot of facts about God and about his dealings with the human race. We might know that Adam and Eve had three sons – not just Cain and Abel, but also Seth. We might know about a man in the Old Testament called Benaiah who fell into a pit on a snowy day. We might know about people like Ehud and Eglon and other obscure figures. The Bible is full of interesting things, and all of it is worth knowing, but the chief purpose of the Bible is to point us to Jesus. The whole of the history of the Jews was leading up to the coming of Jesus, the promised Messiah. The Old Testament records that preparation for Jesus, and the New Testament tells us about the birth, death and resurrection of the Messiah and the birth of his church. The written Word of God speaks to us primarily about Jesus, the Living Word of God, who was with God in the beginning. Knowing the Bible back to front does not necessarily get us to know Jesus unless we read it with an attitude of expectancy.

Jesus was saying to the Jews of his day, 'Your Scriptures, from Genesis through to Malachi, are speaking to you about me, the Messiah. Come to know me through them; don't just treat them as a dry, academic exercise.' When today we read the Bible we should not do it just to learn more biblical facts; we should read it to discover more about Jesus. We should expect to meet a Person, not just to understand a book.

Who do you want to please the most?

Jesus said,

I do not accept praise from men, but I know you ... How can you believe if you accept praise from one another, yet make no effort to obtain the praise that comes from the only God?

(John 5:41–42, 44)

Jesus was saying to the Jews, 'The fundamental question is, who do you want to please the most? Do you want to please God or do you want to please other people?'

Jesus gives us the example we need: he always put God first. He obeyed God, and if people didn't like the consequences of his obedience, that was just too bad. In effect he was saying to the people of his day, 'I don't want your praise – I'm not interested in it one way or another. My behaviour is not conditioned by your opinion of me; it is conditioned by God.' We should have the same attitude: we should prefer being disapproved of by people to being disapproved of by God. As Christians our primary concern should be to please God rather than people.

Where Jesus saw sin and hypocrisy, he had the courage to challenge it. I believe there was a little twinkle in his eye sometimes when he said or did things which he knew were going to disturb people. Scripture calls him the 'rock of offence' (Romans 9:33, King James Version). People were frequently offended by the things Jesus said and did. They would stumble over the Rock and become upset, and then Jesus would have his opportunity to move into their lives and change them. So offending people is not always wrong: sometimes our obedience to God is bound to offend.

All of us try to please people to some degree. Those of us who are married try to please our spouses; parents try to please their children and vice-versa. Church leaders are under pressure to please their congregations. Politicians try to please their voters. Trying to please other people can be a good thing if our motivation is genuine love and kindness, but often we try to please them for less commendable reasons. We may try to please family members in order to have a semblance of peace in the home. Ministers may try to please their church members in order to have an easy time of it.

Too many church leaders let their desire to please people interfere with their obedience to God. Because they know a certain message will be unpopular, they may be tempted to water it down a little, or even to drop it altogether. Sometimes it is necessary for preachers to say uncomfortable things. Preachers will often have to challenge sin and hypocrisy. Sometimes this will get them into trouble, because people never enjoy having their sin pointed out to them. And yet Christian leaders are called to please God first, and then to please people only if this does not interfere with pleasing God.

We all need to ask ourselves, 'Who do I want to please the most?' Whose opinion of us matters more than anyone else's? Can we truly say that we want to please God the most? Or does God have to compete with our families, friends and workmates? Who is the biggest influence on our behaviour? What is the chief motivation in our lives? Is it a desire to obey God or a fear of people and a wish to have an easy life? At work, are we afraid that if we really stand up for Jesus and refuse to compromise our commitment to him we will be branded as religious fanatics? At home, do we give in to wrong pressures from others so that we don't have to cope with any conflict? We should not seek conflict for its own sake, but sometimes we have to face it. So often we want to please a whole range of people first, and then if God is pleased by what we're doing as well, all the better – but the people tend to come first, with God being allowed a minor part in the discussion!

Pleasing his Father was Jesus' number one priority. However, there was no arrogance in his attitude. He wanted to obey God always; that didn't mean that he wanted to offend people just for the sake of it. He loved people and wanted friendship, but he had first of all to obey God. There are a few Christians who, frankly, do offend people just for the sake of it, when it is not necessary to offend them, when there is nothing really wrong with what they are doing. Admittedly, such Christians do try to obey God, but they also needlessly hurt and alienate other people. They may even think their unpopularity is proof that they are obeying God. It may be true that people dislike them partly because they are challenged and offended by their obedience to God, but part of the unpopularity may also be due to rudeness, tactlessness and arrogance. Obeying God is not meant to make us impossible to live with!

Chapter 13

DIVINE RESOURCES

... Jesus crossed to the far shore of the Sea of Galilee ... and a great crowd of people followed him because they saw the miraculous signs he had performed on the sick ... The Jewish passover Feast was near.

When Jesus looked up and saw a great crowd coming towards him, he said to Philip, 'Where shall we buy bread for these people to eat?' He asked this only to test him, for he already had in mind what he was going to do.

Philip answered him, 'Eight months' wages would not buy enough bread for each one to have a bite!'

Another of his disciples, Andrew, Simon Peter's brother, spoke up, 'Here is a boy with five small barley loaves and two small fish, but how far will they go among so many?'

Jesus said, 'Make the people sit down' ... Jesus then took the loaves, gave thanks, and distributed to those who were seated as much as they wanted. He did the same with the fish.

(John 6:1–13)

The other three gospels tell us that Jesus and the disciples had been on a preaching tour and had *crossed to the far shore of the Sea of Galilee* (John 6:1) for a short period of rest and recuperation. However, Jesus' departure did not go unnoticed, *and a great crowd of people followed him because they saw the miraculous signs he had performed on the sick.*

(verse 2)

They were not interested in Jesus as a Saviour from their sin but only as a worker of miracles. Their motivation for following him was mainly curiosity; they wanted to see more signs and wonders.

John mentions that it was Passover time (verse 4). This is significant, because the Passover would have reminded the people of their release from the Egyptian oppression, and they would have been wondering if Jesus was the one who was going to free them from the Roman oppression in a kind of new Passover.

Having gone up on the hillside with his disciples, *Jesus ... saw a great crowd coming towards him* (verse 5). Mark's Gospel tells us that when he saw them

he had compassion on them, because they were like sheep without a shepherd.

(Mark 6:34)

Matthew 14:14 says that

he had compassion on them and healed their sick

while Luke tells us that

He welcomed them and spoke to them about the kingdom of God, and healed those who needed healing.

(Luke 9:11)

How would we have reacted in a similar situation? Suppose we had set aside a few hours for some much-needed peace and quiet, and suddenly a crowd of people turn up needing our attention and help. How would we feel on a Sunday afternoon, after a hard week's work, if an entire church congregation came to our house, wanting teaching and prayer? Jesus did not react by saying, 'Come back when I've had some rest' – that's the sort of thing we might say, isn't it? He had compassion on these people. Even though most of them were only looking for miracles, he saw that they were needy people.

It was getting late in the day and this great crowd of people had walked a long way around the Sea of Galilee and needed something to eat. So Jesus asked Philip, *Where shall we buy bread for these people to eat?* John tells us that

He asked this only to test him, for he already had in mind what he was going to do.

(verse 6)

Jesus wasn't asking Philip where the nearest bakery was; he wanted to know if Philip's outlook had been changed by being with him all this time and seeing the miracles. Had Philip learned that Jesus was truly the Son of God and was quite capable of rising to the occasion with a miracle? Had Philip noted Jesus' compassion for the crowd? Had Philip grasped that Jesus was willing and able to supply the people's needs, the most immediate of which was food? Jesus' mother Mary had perhaps grasped the truth about Jesus. At the wedding at Cana she had said to the servants, *Do whatever he tells you,* knowing that Jesus was capable of a miracle. Had a similar kind of faith yet developed in Philip?

Sadly, no, it seems. Instead of trusting Jesus, he started doing some sums and declared,

Eight months' wages would not buy enough bread for each one to have a bite!

(verse 7)

Matthew tells us that the disciples said,

'Send the crowds away, so they can go to the villages and buy

themselves some food.' Jesus replied, 'They do not need to go away. You give them something to eat.'

(Matthew 14:15–16)

The rest of the disciples were no better than Philip – they didn't suppose that Jesus could do something miraculous, despite all the miracles they had already seen.

But then Andrew spoke up:

Here is a boy with five small barley loaves and two small fish, but how far will they go among so many?

(verse 9)

It is fitting that the unbelief of the adult disciples was quietly rebuked by the little contribution which a child made. Jesus did not reprove the disciples but told them, *Make the people sit down* (verse 10).

John's Gospel records this astonishing miracle in a simple, unpretentious way: Jesus took the five small loaves, gave thanks, and distributed to those who were seated (*i.e.* about five thousand people) as much as they wanted, and then he did the same with the two small fish (verse 11). Human calculation had failed, but Jesus' divine provision did what human resources could never do.

Most of us will be familiar with the dubious explanations of this miracle. Some commentators try to explain it away by saying that what really happened was that the little lad with his loaves and fishes shamed all the adults into bringing out the food which they had until then concealed. The idea is that everyone had thought to bring packed lunches! This is not an interpretation of the passage – it is a rewriting of it! Modern sceptics can say what they like about it, but the disciples knew that they had witnessed a miracle, and so did the five thousand people!

Like the disciples, when faced with challenging

112

situations we often fail to respond with faith. Demands are made on us: perhaps someone wants our time or our money or our commitment or our prayer, and we know that our human resources are totally inadequate. And so we reject the request that has been made of us; we send the person away or we extricate ourselves from the demanding situation we have found ourselves in. We close our eyes to the needs of others because we just can't supply them ourselves. But when we want to do this Jesus' reply to us is, 'You give them something; you do something.' And when we step out in faith and try to meet the needs, trusting that Jesus will supply everything we require to do so, we will see his divine provision at work. In ourselves we do not have the resources to meet the need, but Jesus himself will supply them. He does not ask us to do anything that he will not enable us to do.

Passover fever

After the people saw the miraculous sign that Jesus did, they began to say: 'Surely this is the Prophet who is to come into the world.' Jesus, knowing that they intended to come and make him king by force, withdrew again to a mountain by himself.

(verses 14–15)

They realized that Jesus was the Messiah, but their idea of what the Messiah was like was very far from the truth. They wanted Jesus to be an earthly king who would defeat the hated Roman oppressors for them. But Jesus had not come to be that sort of king. If he allowed them to make him a political figure, he would not be able to perform the great task he had come to do on earth – that is, to be the Saviour of mankind, dying on a cross and rising from the dead.

The crowd was buzzing with a kind of Passover political-religious fever, and it was probably infecting the disciples too. They were beginning to think thoughts like, 'The people want to make Jesus their king ... And if he were king, we would all be princes ... This is getting really exciting!' But Jesus acted decisively to put an end to all this nonsense. Mark tells us:

Immediately Jesus made his disciples get into the boat and go on ahead of him to Bethsaida, while he dismissed the crowd. After leaving them, he went up on a mountain side to pray.

(Mark 6:45–46)

He wisely separated the disciples from the crowd and by the authority of his word packed the disciples off in a boat and sent the people away. Then he simply went off into the hills by himself, escaping from the people's feverish excitement.

Jesus walks on the water

Jesus then spent some time alone, praying and thinking. John the Baptist's recent death must have been in his thoughts, and he must also have been thinking that he would very soon have to go back to Jerusalem to face a sacrificial death there.

Meanwhile the disciples, rowing across the sea, were having a very hard time coping with a storm which had blown up. Mark tells us that Jesus

saw the disciples straining at the oars, because the wind was against them. About the fourth watch of the night he went out to them, walking on the lake.

(Mark 6:48)

Jesus, up in the hills, saw the trouble the disciples were in and went out to them. So although he was not physically with them, he had them in his sight; he was watching over them. I believe he was praying for them. This means that although they were being tossed about by the storm and were afraid for their lives, they were in fact perfectly safe. They were safe not only because Jesus was praying for them but also because

114

he had the power to calm the storm, and even to walk on the water to meet them, saying, *It is I; don't be afraid* (John 6:20).

This reminds me of the famous picture entitled *Peace* in which a bird is sitting quite happily in its nest, which has been built right at the end of a long, thin branch of a tree which seems to extend perilously close to a huge, thundering waterfall. The bird seems to be in great danger, but it is not afraid because it knows the branch is supporting it. It has peace of mind, despite the noise of the mighty waterfall. That is the sort of peace which God wants to give us. It is not the peace which results from being removed from the world, from any potential danger or threat or pressure; it is the peace of knowing that God is looking after us, no matter what may be happening around us or to us. It is the peace of knowing that Jesus is always interceding for us; he never slumbers or sleeps. Because of this we are always safe. He is always looking after us, and so he can say to us, *Do not worry* (Matthew 6:31) and *Do not let your hearts be troubled and do not be afraid* (John 14:27). Right in the middle of the storms of life, Jesus wants us to have his peace, to enjoy freedom from anxiety.

Jesus comes to us and he says, *It is I; don't be afraid*. We can trust Jesus. We may be afraid of temptation, but Jesus says to us, 'I will give you an escape, a way out of every temptation.' We may be afraid of trials, but Jesus says, 'The trials you face build up your patience and character and hope.' We may be afraid of the pressure of work, but Jesus says, 'I will give you rest. Take on my yoke.' We may be afraid of trouble and tribulation, but Jesus says, 'These are necessary for entering the kingdom.' We may be perplexed about the journey which God has given us to travel, but Jesus says, 'I will be your guide.' We may be afraid of the dark storm, but Jesus says, 'I will calm it and I will be with you right in

115

the midst of it.' We may be afraid of the great, swelling waves of persecution, but Jesus says, 'Blessed are those who are persecuted for me.' We may be afraid of death, but Jesus says, 'I will give you eternal life. I will raise you up on the last day. I will be with you.'

Living in two worlds

The thing which stands out in John chapter 6 is that Jesus was operating on a different plane to the disciples. He had different resources, different knowledge, different reactions, a different prayer life, different behaviour and different ambitions. When the disciples were wanting some rest and the crowds came, Jesus didn't try to send them away but responded to them with compassion. When considering how to feed the people, Jesus' reaction was not to calculate how many months' wages it would cost but to look to heaven for a miracle. When faced with the crowd's and the disciples' wish to make him their king, he rejected it and dismissed them all with his divine authority, going off into the hills by himself to pray. Jesus' whole manner was characterized by authority, compassion, wisdom, knowledge and truth.

The disciples misunderstood him; they were slow learners, but he graciously persevered with them, patiently teaching them his way. This means that there is hope for us too: Jesus is patient with us and will continue to teach us. We can learn to imitate his behaviour; we can learn to live and work as he did. He was both human and divine; he lived both in heaven and in the world. He wants us to live in two worlds also: our values and power are to come from heaven, and we are to work in this world, manifesting God's kingdom in it. Jesus said that we were to do even greater works than he had done during his earthly ministry (see John 14:12). In order to do the things he did in the way he did them, we need to have resources, knowledge, reactions, prayers, behaviour and ambitions which have their origin in another realm – in the kingdom of God.